SANTA CLAUS BANK ROBBERY

A TRUE-CRIME SAGA IN TEXAS

TUI SNIDER

About the Author

Tui Snider is an award-winning author, speaker, photographer, and musician specializing in North Texas travel, cemetery symbolism, quirky history, and haunted places. As she puts it, "I used to write fiction – but then, I moved to Texas!"

Tui has worn a lot of hats in her life - literally - and is especially fond of berets. Her writing and photography have been featured by numerous outlets, including Coast to Coast AM, WFAA TV, *LifeHack*, *Authentic Texas*, Cult of Weird, and Lone Star Literary Life. Tui loves giving presentations and occasionally teaches classes based on her books at TCU in Fort Worth.

Snider's published books include *Unexpected Texas, Paranormal Texas, Understanding Cemetery Symbols, 100 Things to Do in Dallas - Fort Worth Before You Die, Twitter for Writers*, and more. Tui has several more books in progress. You can find all of Tui's books by visiting her Amazon Author Page: http://bit.ly/TuiBooks.

Tui loves connecting with readers all over the globe on social media as @TuiSnider and through her website: TuiSnider.com. So don't be shy; say hi!

Dedication

To Larry, who knows that getting lost is often the best way to find things.

Acknowledgments

Whether you helped with technical problems, shared information, or simply offered a kind word at the right time, I couldn't have completed the *Santa Claus Bank Robbery* without the encouragement and assistance I received from the following:

Dr. Duane K. Hale, Hall Ways, John Waggoner, Banjo Billy, Sheriff Wayne Bradford, Rhyne Hobbs, Candice Piper, Julie Williams Coley, Owen Lean, Patricia Lynne, StoryDam Twitter chat peeps, David Sumoflam Kravetz, Joy Daley, Naomi Morlan, Andy Hoenninger, SJ MacMillan, Eddie Hargrave, Tracey Walsh, Sarah Twidal, Tara Augenstein, Bob and Connie McIntyre, Steve Cameron, Pete and Margaret Cameron, Sharon Furrer, Ian McAllister, Alycia Forbes, Anne Bray, Nicole Rivera, Rose Ketring, Gus Pegel, Michael Snidersich, Sean Grose, Ronnie Whennen, NellyBelle, Jan Gomes, Ed Goodson, GhostCat, Tracy Fox Olson, Gonna Blevins, Russell & Penny Andrews, Heidi Fountain, Lisa Listwa, Jessica Wilson, Michael Samyn, Julie Reeser, Woof Mutt, Teal Gray, Miss Otis...

...and whoever those friendly folks were who anonymously paid for our meal that day in Sweetwater, Texas!

Table of Contents

Chapter 1
Setting the Scene

An Unexpected Diner

My fascination with the Santa Claus bank robbery was triggered by a home style meal in an unexpected diner, or as I like to say, "Santa found me when I was lost in West Texas." As a writer, I'm always on the lookout for offbeat stories and overlooked places. I got a whole heap of both on a road trip my husband and I took in March of 2012.

Whether traveling back roads or taking the highway, Larry and I seek Mom and Pop places at mealtimes. This particular day, as lunchtime came and went, we struggled to find a ghost town, let alone a McDonald's. Cell phone coverage can be spotty in West Texas and even with maps and a reliable GPS, getting lost was a real possibility.

My iPhone finally scraped up enough cell power to use Yelp, a travel app that steered us to a nondescript house in the outskirts of Sweetwater. Aside from a small "open" sign in the window, little indicated that this was a public restaurant and not a private residence.

As we parked, I mentally composed an apology for barging into a stranger's home, just in case. Even after stepping in, I worried we'd crashed a family gathering because tables were pushed together with everyone dining side by side. It wasn't until I noticed framed restaurant reviews on the walls from the likes of Texas Monthly, D Magazine, and other publications that I began to relax.

Seeing our hesitation, the server pointed to some empty seats. "There's a couple spots by Junior," she called from the kitchen. "Go on and seat yourself."

As we settled in, I wondered who Junior could be. I didn't have to wonder long; a man in a cowboy hat introduced himself while passing a big bowl of fried chicken our way. "Y'all gotta try the squash, too," he told us. "They grow it out back."

"Homestyle cooking" is a common restaurant claim but at Allen Family Style Meals, this well-worn phrase actually means something. I truly felt at home. Not at my home, mind you, but at the home of some distant West Texas relative about whom I'd only ever heard rumors. The atmosphere was casual, friendly, and unpretentious. There's no menu. You simply pass dishes around the table and take what you want as if dining at a friend's house. Larry and I don't even know the price because someone surreptitiously picked up our tab!

When our tablemates learned I was a writer and that we had just visited Eastland one of them asked, "Did you see where they lynched Santa Claus?"

"What?" I replied, figuring I had misheard.

As the rest of the table chimed in with what they knew about this absurd-sounding event, I eagerly took notes. What started as a segment in my first travel book (*Unexpected Texas*) eventually grew into a book project.

I've been researching the West Texas lynching of Santa Claus ever since. Not only is it a real event, but the more I look, the more unexpected twists and turns I uncover regarding this strange-but-true piece of history.

A.C. Greene's book

Anyone who researches the lynching of Santa Claus quickly discovers A.C. Greene's book. First released in 1972, *The Santa Claus Bank Robbery* is a gripping page-turner that reads like a novel. This is because the author invents conversations and makes assumptions about the bandits' and victims' thoughts and feelings. The end result is very entertaining.

Although Greene's book is well-written, many readers, including historians and news reporters, forget that it is a fictionalized account. During my own research, I was shocked to find that Greene uses fictitious names for several key figures.

Unfortunately, Greene's book is often used as the sole source for annual retellings about this infamous crime. Since so many accounts in books and magazines are based on A.C. Greene's novel I struggled to verify certain aspects of his information. After all, searching newspaper archives for *fake* names is not going to yield any *real* information. Without real names, my research kept hitting dead ends. It was frustrating! I couldn't shake the feeling that something was off.

Separating Fact from Fiction

A major breakthrough came when I found Julie Williams Coley's book, *How Did They Die?* which chronicles high profile murders and infamous deaths in North Texas. Coley's book is hefty and meticulously researched. Unlike Greene's book, it is a straightforward recounting of facts with little embroidery.

However, it was from Coley's chapter on the Santa Claus Bank Robbery that I finally learned the *real* names of people connected to the infamous heist, along with other helpful facts. Thanks to these leads, my research took off.

In addition to Coley's book, I owe a lot to Dr. Duane K. Hale, John Waggoner, Sheriff Wayne Bradford, Billy Smith, and Rhyne Hobbs. Each of them offered indispensable insight along the way.

Every version of the Santa Claus Bank Robbery, even from eye-witnesses, contains variations, however slight. I based this book on the most accurate sources I could find. While I hope the story keeps readers' attention, it is not a novelized account. Quotes included have appeared in courtroom testimony, newspaper archives, eye-witness interviews, or reliable books. I've enjoyed scouring for anecdotes and historical facts to weave into this book.

Even after several years of research, I am still not finished with this story. The more I dig, the less convinced I am that all criminals involved in the Santa Claus Bank Robbery were brought to justice. In my opinion, there was an additional participant, someone who may have even gotten away with murder. Read on, and see what you think!

KANSAS CITY

KANSAS CITY, April 8. (Exclusive)—A machine gun turret of heavy steel with bullet-proof glass windows was erected in the City Bank here today, to give bandits a taste of their own medicine. Several weeks ago a dozen "cowboy" bandits staged a rodeo at the bank and escaped with more than $50,000 in cash.

Los Angeles Times, April 9, 1928

The 1920s: Age of Bank Robberies

You may be surprised to learn that the infamous Santa Claus bank robbery occurred during the Roaring Twenties and not during the Wild West Era. Despite Hollywood's portrayal, bank robberies were a rare occurrence on the early frontier. Jesse James' gang kicked things off with the first U.S. bank robbery in 1866, but until 1900 fewer than a dozen were reported. In frontier days, most financial institutions found that a good solid safe was the only protection they needed. However, I did read about a particularly paranoid banker in Oklahoma who kept patrons' money in a cage full of live rattlesnakes.

This lack of Wild West bank robberies had nothing to do with a shortage of criminals. Stage coaches and trains simply made easier prey than fortified buildings in the heart of town. As automobiles became more common, the dynamic changed completely. Combined with a wider network of passable roads, cars enabled bandits to drive into city centers, dash into crowded banks, raid vaults, and make a quick getaway.

To Have Gas Protection — The new City National Bank & Trust company is amply provided with burglar protection. Inset in the front of each teller's cage there is a camouflaged tear gas gun which is operated by the teller in the cage stepping on a trigger, which releases the gas from the guns into the face of any intruder in the main lobby of the bank. Each man is equipped with a revolver for emergency use, it is stated. One of the officials has a fountain pen, which is seemingly innocent, but which releases tear gas.

Battle Creek Enquirer, August 24, 1929

Several Bank Robberies Every Day in Texas

By the 1920s, oil boomtowns dotted otherwise unpopulated regions throughout Texas. These towns often employed only a handful of law enforcement agents. Few police cars had radios, making it tough to coordinate car chases and set up roadblocks during hot pursuit. Criminals soon realized that a decent getaway car made boomtown banks ripe for plunder. Put all these variables together and here's what you get: By the mid-1920s, the state of Texas experienced three to four bank robberies every single day!

By now, that banker who kept live rattlesnakes in his vault probably felt rather smug as other bankers took their own desperate measures. In Nevada, for instance, businessman George Wingfield, who owned a banking chain there, made a big show of handing out shotguns and ammo to every single cashier in his employ.

Tear Gas Guns were All the Rage

Business owners and law enforcement agents began experimenting with tear gas to repel bandits. This became such a fad during the 1920s that newspapers from the era are riddled with tear gas mishaps. It's hard to say how many robberies were diverted by its use. Some banks gave tellers tear gas canisters disguised as fountain pens for protection. Unfortunately, these were often triggered when bank customers mistook the items for real pens.

In Arizona, a bank installed tear gas guns above its

TEAR GAS GUN EXPLODES; HITS SHERIFF IN EYE

News-Herald, Franklin, PA May 4, 1928

teller cages. This may have deterred bandits, but after several law-abiding customers were sprayed, it also deterred business.

After losing more than $50,000 in a heist, City Bank in Kansas City, Missouri fought fire with fire by placing a machine gun turret directly over its bank vault. According to the public statement, "The bank guard will be equipped with a Thompson sub-machine gun, the same type the bandits used to terrorize those in the bank at the time of the recent hold up.

Rewards for Dead Bank Robbers

Many states, including Oklahoma, Nevada, Illinois, and Nebraska, began offering rewards for captured

MONEY REWARD

For DEAD Bank Robbers

A cash reward will be paid for each Bank Robber legally killed while Robbing this bank

THE Texas Bankers Association, a corporation, offers a standing reward for each bank robber legally killed while robbing and holding up a reward subscribing member bank in Texas with firearms during the daytime. Limits of the place and time of such killing are: in the banking house, or as the robbers and holdups leave the bank, while the robbery and holdup and threats are being committed within the bank; and as they flee from the bank with the property taken, and are resisting legal pursuit and arrest, within five miles of the bank robbed and within one hour after the robbery and holdup.

The amount of the reward for each dead robber will be the total collected from subscribing member banks at $5 per subscriber, but the total amount, in any event, shall not exceed $5,000.00.

This reward does not apply to night attacks on Texas banks.

The Association will not give one cent for live bank robbers. They are rarely identified, more rarely convicted, and most rarely stay in the penitentiary when sent there—all of which operations are troublesome, burdensome and costly to our government.

In order to protect the lives of people in such banks and to protect the property of such banks, the Association is prepared to pay for any number of such robbers and holdups so killed, while they are robbing and holding up its reward subscribing member banks with firearms in the daytime.

It is expressly provided that only the Texas Bankers Association shall determine whether or not payment of this reward shall be made hereunder, and to whom (if anyone) such payment shall be made, and such determination and judgment shall be final, conclusive and not reviewable.

This reward is effective January 15th, 1933, and all other rewards, offers and statements are cancelled and superseded hereby.

TEXAS BANKERS ASSOCIATION

(poster courtesy of the Lela Latch Lloyd Museum)

bank robbers. While a few of these states offered money for live bank robbers, *dead* bank robbers were worth much more in every case.

Eventually, the Texas State Bankers Association increased its $500 robber bounty to an all-time high. In a proclamation released November 9, 1927, the association stated that, "Until further notice the Association will pay $5,000 for each person shot down in the act of robbing one of our banks." For the sake of clarity, the statement added, "We want dead bandits and no other kind." To put this in perspective, the average annual wage in the 1920s was less than $1,500!

Daily Sentinel, Rome, NY, Mar 12, 1928

Chapter 2
Key Players

A Pair of Kindhearted Women

In 1926, brothers Marshall and Lee Ratliff robbed a bank in Valera, a West Texas town about 60 miles southwest of Cisco. The robbery went smoothly, and the duo made off with a cool $9,000. They might have gotten away with the heist, but instead of keeping low, they gambled, drank, and most importantly, bragged about their escapade. As word spread, the guys were caught, convicted, and promptly sent off to prison, where they would have remained for many years had it not been for a pair of kindhearted women.

The first of these was the Ratliff boys' mother, Nancy Jerilla Carter. Rilla, as she was known, operated the Manhattan Café in Cisco. She and her boys were well-known around town, so Rilla quickly drummed up enough support to petition the governor for her sons' early release.

With Miriam "Ma" Ferguson as the current governor of Texas, Rilla's timing could not have been better. Aside from being the second female governor in

U.S. history, Ferguson pardoned an average of 100 criminals every month. (Her predecessor, meanwhile, granted a mere 297 pardons during his entire four-year term.)

Ma Ferguson's reputation was so well- known that a convict once broke out of jail, and rather than run for the border, he showed up at the governor's mansion in Austin to request his pardon in person. True to form,

Miriam "Ma" Ferguson (photo source: Wikimedia Commons)

the softhearted governor granted his wish, but she made him report back to jail first.

A running joke through Ferguson's governorship went something like this: A man accidentally bumps into Ma Ferguson and says, "Governor, I beg your pardon," to which she replies, "I will, son. Just give me a few minutes for the paperwork." By the end of her second term, Ferguson had granted nearly 4,000 pardons, a record that remains unbroken by any other Texas governor to this day.

TWO PARDONS, THREE FURLOUGHS GRANTED BY GOV. FERGUSON

Two conditional pardons and three furloughs have been granted by Governor Miriam A. Ferguson in three and a half days in office.

Texas Gov. Miriam "Ma" Ferguson was well-known for granting pardons to prisoners. (Austin American Sun, Jan 25, 1925.)

How the Santa Claus Gangsters Met

Included in Ferguson's many pardons were a couple for Rilla Carter's boys. That's how, after serving less than a year of their lengthy sentences, Marshall and Lee Ratliff were free men once more by mid-1927.

The Texas State Penitentiary is located in Huntsville, a good 300 miles from Cisco, so it's doubtful the Ratliff brothers had many visitors from home. During their brief prison stint, however, Lee and Marshall befriended a couple inmates who also hailed from West Texas, namely Henry Helms and Robert Hill.

Rilla Carter (photo courtesy of the Conrad Hilton Center)

Henry Helms with his wife, Nettie. (photo courtesy of the Conrad Hilton Center.)

Santa Claus Gang Member: Henry Helms

Although married with children, Henry Helms was hardly a family man. With pastimes including car theft, bootlegging, burglary, and dealing drugs, this preacher's son was more sinner than saint. However, Helms was the only one with a home to return to after the four men were pardoned in 1927.

Helms also knew of a boarding house willing to rent to ex-cons, so the Ratliff brothers and Robert Hill followed him to Wichita Falls.

Sympathetic Boarding House

The boarding house to which Helms directed his friends was owned by an electrician and his wife, Mr. and Mrs. Francis and Josephine Herron. The Herrons took in boarders to make ends meet, but they got more than they bargained for with the Helms' gang.

Francis Herron didn't mind the Ratliff boys or Robert Hill too much, although they made him uneasy. Henry Helms, on the other hand, truly scared him. According to Mr. Herron, 30-year-old Helms was a quick-tempered bully who fired his pistol near people's shoes to get his point across. "When Helms ordered anybody to do anything, they obeyed right then or took the chance of getting their feet shot off," he claimed. "When he talked, everybody listened."

Things got so bad that Mr. Herron quietly sent at least one of his teen-aged daughters to stay with relatives. Her absence, however, greatly upset the Helms' gang. One of them even said he planned to marry her. While that remark may have been a joke, Henry Helms' reaction was not. He gave Mr. Herron an ultimatum, and when his landlord hesitated, Helms shot at his feet. Fearing for his life, Mr. Herron promptly brought the girl back home.

The First Fake Names Emerge

In A.C. Greene's book, the landlords at the boarding house are called Freeman and Midge Tellet. While they actually had two teenaged daughters, Greene only mentions one, who he gives the fictitious name of Rheba.

If you find this rather strange, you are not alone! At the end of his book, Greene admits to adding in a few fictitious touches to flesh out his narrative. Since he wanted the book to read like a novel, this certainly makes sense. However, Greene never once reveals that he uses pseudonyms for several people in his book.

Greene's book mentions the exact same newspaper interviews with "Midge Tellet" that I later read. I recognize the quotes. However, newspapers from that time always refer to her as Josephine Herron and never as Midge Tellet. Keep this in mind as the tale unfolds!

Santa Claus Gang Member: Robert Hill

Robert Hill was the youngest member of the gang. Hill spent most of his childhood in a state-run reformatory, but not through any fault of his own. Orphaned at age 10, the poor kid was institutionalized with delinquents not through any misdeeds of his own, but simply due to a lack of options.

Robert Hill met the other guys while serving time in Huntsville prison. At 21, Hill had never married and had no family. After his rough start in life, he wasn't out for thrills or rebellion. He simply wanted a load of cash so he could move far away and start a brand new life.

Santa Gang Member: Marshall Ratliff

Aside from his prison record, 24-year-old Marshall

Marshall Ratliff and his wife, Mattie Belle. Can you see the strong resemblance between Marshall and his father, Lee Roy? (photo courtesy of the Conrad Hilton Center.)

Marshall Ratliff is on the far right, with his father, Lee Roy, in the middle of the children. The two men look so similar that this photo is often mislabeled. (photo courtesy of the Conrad Hilton Center.)

Ratliff had a lot going for him. He was a handsome fellow, known for a good singing voice, generosity, and sense of humor.

In 1921, Marshall Ratliff married Mattie Belle Minica. The couple had two sons, but after his prison release they no longer lived together, and she eventually remarried.

The physical resemblance between Marshall and his father is so strong that photos of Lee Roy Ratliff are often mistakenly identified as Marshall. Since Lee Roy also walked away from a wife and two young sons, it appears that the father and son were alike in deed as well as looks.

Fateful Choices

At this point, it seems like those four young men could have carved out a low-key yet law-abiding life after prison. Whether or not they actually tried that approach is hard to tell. As you will soon see, such an attempt could not have lasted long. Marshall later complained that as ex-cons they had trouble finding legitimate work. As for Marshall's brother, Lee, by November 1927, he was back in jail for another robbery.

Tui Snider

Chapter 3
Easy Money

Ratliff's Get Rich Quick Scheme

While Henry Helms is often cited as the gang's leader, robbing Cisco's First National Bank was Marshall Ratliff's brainchild. After living there for several years, Ratliff knew the town's weak spots.

Cisco's First National Bank was in the middle town, prominently located along Avenue D. This was Cisco's main drag, a wide street paved in red bricks from the nearby town of Thurber. In those days, when locals spoke of "Main Street" they were referring to "Avenue D."

The First National Bank building had previously been a retail store, and large glass display windows still flanked its entrance. The interior had been remodeled to suit the needs of a bank. The president and cashier had open-air offices partitioned by waist-high walls on the left hand side. A series of teller cages continued down the left side, while a counter where customers stood to prepare paperwork ran down the right side. The bank kept its bookkeeping office in a closed off room along the back wall. (See page 36 for diagram of the bank layout.)

None of these features mattered much to Marshall Ratliff. Cisco's First National Bank wasn't even the biggest bank in town. What attracted Ratliff was a door in the bank's back office that opened onto a side alley. That alley made all the difference in the world.

Although not an official through-street, this side-alley often served as a shortcut for drivers and pedestrians heading to Main Street. Shoppers sometimes used the alley for parking, so a getaway car near the bank's side door would not seem suspicious, especially on a busy Friday afternoon. Taken together, these little details made Cisco's First National Bank ideal for an easy heist.

What could possibly go wrong?

The bandits figured that the Friday before Christmas was perfect for a hold up, but they needed at least four men to pull it off. Since Lee Ratliff was back in jail, they cast about for other members. It didn't take Henry Helms long to find the perfect man, an experienced safecracker who knew his way around a bank vault. Unfortunately, this man, whose name I've yet to find, caught the flu and had to drop out.

Santa Gang Member: Lewis Davis

At the last minute, Henry Helms enlisted his brother-in-law to round out the crew. At 32, Lewis Davis was the oldest member of the robbery gang, but he had the least criminal experience.

Unlike the other three, Davis was a genuine family man with a steady job and no criminal record. He had a wife, two kids, and worked in a Wichita Falls' glass factory. However, with bills stacking up, a family to support, and maybe even a bit of persuasion from Henry Helms, Lewis agreed to the caper. Much like Robert Hill, Lewis Davis viewed the robbery as a one-time opportunity to better his station in life.

Good Disguise for a Bad Man

After gathering his team, a major dilemma loomed; while Helms, Hill, and Davis were strangers who could blend into the crowd, people in Cisco knew Ratliff's face, and even worse, his reputation. How could he approach the bank without being recognized? To make matters worse, the bank's cashier, Alex Spears, was one of the folks who helped Ratliff's mom arrange his pardon for the Valera heist. Unbeknownst to Ratliff, Spears had also recently led a campaign to provide local police with riot guns, with the obvious implication that they be used against bank robbers.

While puzzling over this, Ratliff noticed his landlady, Mrs. Josephine Herron, sewing a Santa suit for her husband to wear on Christmas Day. This gave Ratliff an idea. Rather than tie a handkerchief around his face, he could enter the bank wearing a Santa Suit. This would conceal his identity without arousing suspicions.

On Thursday, December 22, 1927 Ratliff, Helms, Hill, and Davis pulled up to the Herron home in a blue Buick sedan. Although the bandits claimed the car was owned by Davis, they had stolen it from a wealthy oilman. This Buick was a fancy rig, with wood trim and gray cloth upholstery. The back seat windows featured roller shades with cut glass flower vases.

Red Flags for Josephine Herron

At dinner, the men told Josephine Herron they were taking a road trip later that night. The landlady knew better than to ask questions, but she must have suspected they were up to more than their usual bootlegging runs.

Herron later testified that not only did the men send her to the store for iodine, bandages, and canned food, but they made an unusual request. According to her, Henry Helms told her that if anything should happen to him, he wanted her to send a doctor named J.T. Vick down to his sister-in-law's ranch.

Another A. C. Greene Discrepancy

Once again, A. C. Greene omits intriguing details and supplies fake names when covering this part of the story in his narrative. In this case, Greene fails to mention that Helms' sister-in-law just so happens to be Lewis Davis' sister, Minnie Fox. Nor does he ever mention that Henry Helms was married to another one of Davis' sisters, Nettie Mae.

In other words, the Henry Helms and Lewis Davis are brothers-in-law and A.C. Greene went out of his way to obscure this fact. In addition, Greene uses fictitious names for names for Minnie Fox, as well as Dr. Vick.

Mrs. Herron later told police that the reason she

kept all her information about the gangsters to herself was because her husband "was so free in his talk." At least she had a reason. I don't know what A.C. Greene's excuse is.

Before leaving the boarding house in Wichita Falls, the bandits persuaded Josephine Herron to let Ratliff borrow her Santa suit. It's not clear whether or not Helms used his pistol to convince her. At this point, the Herron family probably knew better than to get on his bad side. It is known that the Santa costume's pants did not fit Ratliff. There wasn't enough time to tailor them, so he only borrowed Santa's mask, hat, and jacket.

The "Santa Claus Gang" clockwise from top left: Marshall Ratliff, Henry Helms, Lewis Davis, Robert Hill (photo courtesy of the Conrad Hilton Center in Cisco.)

Chapter 4
The Robbery

Road to Cisco

Cisco is roughly 150 miles southwest of Wichita Falls, so the men had a long drive. To take the edge off their pre-robbery jitters, they sipped a powerful bootleg whisky called "Electra Lightning" along the way.

Sometime between 2:00 and 3:00 a.m. they arrived at the farm where Lewis Davis' sister, Minnie Fox, lived. The Fox ranch, as the newspapers refer to it, was located near Moran, so it was only 15 miles or so northwest of Cisco.

It wasn't Minnie, however, who greeted the men, but her husband, Mr. Sam Fox. The early-rising rancher was not pleased to be woken by four boozy men in the middle of the night, so he made them stay outside in a tent.

After Sam left for work the next morning, Minnie invited the hungover crew into her home, where she fed them breakfast and coffee. Even though Lewis had never been in trouble with the law, his sister was suspicious. Without giving her specific details, the men let Minnie think her brother was helping them with a lucrative bootlegging run.

Before they left, Lewis promised his sister this was the only crime he would ever commit. Little did the two of them know how true those words would be.

Santa Claus Comes to Town

In the early 20th century, cotton and coal gave West Texas its first taste of prosperity. When the Ranger Oilfield was discovered in 1917, this "black gold" kept the riches flowing. Over the next 10 years as the oil boom faded, agriculture picked up the slack, especially cattle, peanuts, and cotton. By 1927, Cisco's population was a sturdy 15,000, and the city remained an important hub for the region.

Shortly before noon on Friday, December 23, 1927, Ratliff, Helms, Davis, and Hill drove their stolen Buick into the bustling city of Cisco. It was unseasonably warm and the town buzzed with last-minute Christmas shoppers.

To give his companions a feel for Cisco's layout, Ratliff took the men for a quick spin past First National Bank while he crouched low in the back seat. Afterwards, the men dropped Ratliff at the far end of town so he could walk down and meet them at the bank. As predicted, no one paid much attention to Helms, Davis, and Hill as they parked their car in the side alley by First National Bank and waited.

The Pied Piper Effect

Meanwhile, Ratliff, dressed in a festive red coat, red

hat, and Santa mask with a white beard sauntered down Avenue D towards First National Bank."

As expected, Ratliff's outfit disguised him well. The only problem was an unintentional Pied Piper effect. Not only were kids approaching him, but some even followed him down the street. For the most part, Santa played along. However, when a woman asked which

That's Cisco's First National Bank on the left, with people crossing the alley over to Garner's Department Store. As you can also see, people used to park their cars right down the middle of the street. (photo courtesy of the Conrad Hilton Center)

store he was affiliated with, he merely grumbled, "You'll find out soon enough."

Another person who remembered meeting Santa Claus that fateful day was Lela Latch, a college senior home for the holidays. She was strolling down Avenue D with her 6-year-old brother, Bill. After shaking Latch's hand, Santa asked Bill what he wanted for Christmas.

"What? You didn't get my letter?" Bill asked in dismay. When Santa quickly explained that the letter was filed away, Bill reminded him that a football topped his list.

A Less than Jolly St. Nick

After a brisk morning, a pleasant lull had washed over Cisco's First National Bank. President Charlie Fee was home for lunch, leaving his son-in- law, Alex Spears, in charge. Leaning over the low wall of the cashier's office to chat with Spears was his friend Marion Olson, a college student home for Christmas from Harvard Law School. Except for Mr. Jewell Poe, the bank tellers were out to lunch. After taking a deposit from a grocer named Oscar Cliett, Poe and his customer also enjoyed a conversation.

In the back bookkeeping offices, Freda Stroebel and Vance Littleton worked through their lunch hour to catch up from the busy morning. Stroebel had just advised 12-year-old Laverne Comer and 10-year-old Emma Mae Robinson on the proper way to withdraw the money that Laverne earned raising calves. The two little girls were headed for the front door when in walked Santa Claus.

As all eyes turned towards the jolly man in the red suit, three men slipped in behind him. They did not seem affiliated with Santa, so no one paid much

*Here's what Cisco's First Nation Bank looked like circa 1927.
(photo courtesy of the Conrad Hilton Center.)*

attention to them.

Alex Spears was first to speak, addressing the costumed man with a hearty, "Hello, Santa Claus!" When Santa failed to reply, Spears repeated his greeting. This time Santa answered, but it was a muffled grunt rather than clear words. Ratliff likely feared Spears would recognize his voice.

While customers assumed Santa's appearance was a holiday prank, Spears grew increasingly uneasy. Boomtown or not, Cisco was small enough that he knew most customers by name. Before Spears could interrogate Santa further, the trio behind Ratliff pulled out guns. One of the armed men approached Poe's teller cage and said, "Stick 'em up."

"What do you mean?" Poe stammered.

"I mean business, big boy," the gunman replied.

Things turned even more sinister as Santa shouted for everyone to "grab some sky" in a less than jolly tone. It was suddenly clear that Santa was on the naughty list, too, and not just the armed men behind him.

As Hill covered Spears and Olson with a pair of pistols, Helms herded Poe and Cliett into the cashier's office by gesturing with his gun. The four hostages were soon lined up against the wall.

Santa Claus stepped into Poe's booth. He rummaged through the drawers until he found the teller's pistol, then tucked it into his pants. Santa told Poe to open the bank's vaults. Once the safe opened, Santa yanked a sack from beneath his red jacket and began stuffing it with money. An uneasy silence gripped the room as everyone waited for the tense ordeal to end.

As seconds ticked by bank customer, Oscar Cliett recalled how his wife, Maureen, often teased him by saying, "Oscar, when you die and meet your maker, you'll have a chew of tobacco in your mouth."

Not wanting to prove her right, Cliett suddenly blurted, "Move over," to Robert Hill, adding that he needed to use the spittoon.

"Spit on the floor," Hill told him. So, he did.

Despite Cliett's outburst, the heist proceeded smoothly. In fact, if things had continued like this, the robbery might have gone off without a hitch.

Chapter 5
The Heist Hits a Snag

Yes Frances, there is a Santa Claus

In this case, the "hitch" came in the form of an exuberant 6-year-old girl named Frances Blasingame. After spying Santa from across the street, Frances begged her mother, Mrs. B.P. Blasingame, to stop by the bank as a treat. Holding her mother's hand, Frances made a beeline for Santa as the pair stepped into First National Bank.

Mrs. Blasingame, however, immediately noticed bank patrons with their hands in the air and a man in front of her brandishing pistols. When she turned to leave, an armed bandit moved to block the front door. Frances spied the guns, too. "They're going to shoot Santa Claus!" she cried out.

As customers stood frozen with their hands over their heads, Mrs. Blasingame and Frances shuffled towards the rear of the bank. Ratliff wasn't the only one who knew about that side door to the alley. Even though bandits yelled for her to stay put or they would shoot, Mrs. Blasingame kept up her momentum.

As the pair breezed through the bookkeeping room,

CHILD'S FAITH IN SANTA PREVENTED ESCAPE OF BANK ROBBERS AFTER CISCO HOLDUP

Corsicana Daily Sun, January 2, 1928

Mrs. Blasingame told Freda Stroebel and Vance Littleton, "They're robbing the bank!"

Mrs. Blasingame and her daughter stepped out the side alley door, turned left, and ran past the getaway car on their way up the alley. Cisco's police station was only one block over, so it didn't take long for her to inform cops of the crime in progress. It's interesting to note that according to Mrs. Blasingame, there were seven or eight gangsters in the bank.

Mrs. Blasingame's courage paid off. Not only was the pair unharmed, but it seems that Saint Nick's character remained untarnished in little Frances' mind. "But really that man was not Old Santa Claus," the little girl later told reporters, "for I saw his pants and they were just like Papa's."

Locals "do the math"

Cisco's chief of police, Mr. George Emory Bedford was a well-respected man known affectionately as "Bit" by local citizens. At 6' foot 4", 220 pounds,

Bedford's physical stature loomed nearly as large as his reputation. With a career spanning over 25 years, Bedford was considered one of the last of the frontier law men, with an ability to maintain order in a manner befitting a western movie. It's often reported that Bedford's mere presence once halted a riot without a single word being spoken – although I have yet to find a historical record of this event.

Peace Officers Make a Plan

Upon hearing Mrs. Blasingame's report, Bedford quickly devised a plan. He told Deputy George W. Carmichael and Officer R.T. Redies to approach the bank from the back side, the same direction Mrs. Blasingame had fled to safety. The two officers could cover the bank's side door while taking cover in the small alley, behind the bank. Bedford, meanwhile, would cover the bank's front door and the section of the alley where it met Main Street.

On his way to the crime scene, Chief Bedford saw Reverend Thomas Lennox walking towards the bank. "They're robbing the bank," Bedford warned. "Get men and guns and block the street."

Local Vigilantes Take Part

Word of the robbery spread quickly, and while some fled the scene, others willingly ran towards it. As sirens blared, business ground to a halt in downtown Cisco. People either took cover or grabbed any weapons they could find. Lela Latch and her brother,

Tui Snider

The Santa Claus Bank Robbery of Cisco's First National Bank

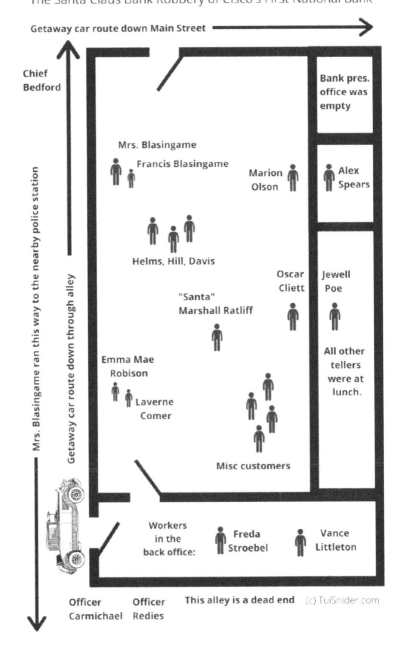

Diagram of Cisco's First National Bank December 23, 1927

Bill, were only a few blocks away when they heard gunfire. At the time, they did not connect this with their Santa Claus encounter.

Latch later recalled, "It was panic. People ran out into the streets with butcher knives, shotguns, anything they could get."

Those who fled the scene remember how frightened they were, while those who raced towards the bank recall a festive air, at least at first. How much of this civic altruism was inspired by the Dead Bank Robber Award is hard to say, but if Mrs. Blasingame was right and there were eight armed bandits, that put a lot of reward money on the line at $5000 a head.

Hardware Store Hands Out Guns

Collins Hardware Store responded to Cisco's emergency by handing out guns and ammo to willing vigilantes as freely as if they were cookies and candy canes. A teenager named Goober Keyes and three of his friends were among those who received free shotguns.

Years later Keyes remarked, "Now wasn't that foolish to give four high school boys guns like that?" before adding, "I really believe that Cisco was a good place for a teenager to be brought up at that time; they had a curfew that was strictly enforced; everyone had to be off the streets by 9 o'clock at night."

Adults offering help included Cisco's postmaster, J.W. Triplett, and his assistant W.P. Coldwell. The two men grabbed their government issued service revolvers and raced to the scene. Coldwell hid behind a big utility pole that shielded him from the bank's back door. Within minutes, a dozen or more armed vigilantes crouched in the alley, waiting to ambush the bandits.

Warning shots?

Despite hearing a few muffled shouts, bank employees, Freda Stroebel and Vance Littleton, had no idea of the robbery in progress until Mrs. Blasingame and Frances burst through the door to their back office. After watching the pair escape, Stroebel was tempted to make a dash for it, too. Littleton, however, warned her to stay put. Stroebel hesitated just long enough to miss her window of opportunity, for just then, Henry Helms stepped into the bookkeeping office with two little girls in tow.

Stroebel later reported that instead of being afraid, she found herself staring at Helms' face, unable to fully believe she was in the middle of a bank robbery. When Helms noticed Stroebel's gaze, he snarled, "Don't look at me like that."

While Santa finished stuffing his burlap sack with loot, Poe cleverly pretended not to notice two bags containing several thousand dollars remaining in the safe, nor did he mention an additional $5000 in his teller's cage. As the two men emerged from the vault, it seemed like the worst was over. The real ordeal was just beginning, however, kicked off by a gunshot through the bank's front windows.

It's often reported that either Ratliff or Helms fired this shot after seeing a curious pedestrian peer into the bank. Others claim this first gunshot was a signal to an unnamed accomplice letting him or her know the robbery was nearly over. What we do know is that shortly after this first shot, one of Cisco's citizens responded by firing a shot back into the bank.

At this, Robert Hill decided to warn the people outside. After loudly announcing that, "I'm going to let them know we are armed," he fired four shots into the ceiling. Hill thought these warning shots would calm things down.

He was dead wrong.

Tui Snider

Chapter 6
A Wild Shootout

Hostages and Human Shields

Instead of defusing the situation, Hill's warning ignited a 15-minute, nonstop fusillade during which at least 200 shots were fired – and that's a conservative estimate. People took cover under tables and desks as bullets flew both into and out of the bank. With surrender out of the question, the robbers realized their safety rested with numbers, so they began shoving the frightened bank hostages towards the bookkeeping room.

With 16 people now crammed into the back room, Santa announced that he expected folks to ride in the getaway car. Spying the bookkeepers huddled beneath a desk, Santa ordered Freda Stroebel to stand up. He then used Stroebel as a human shield by crisscrossing his arms around her chest as the pair made their way toward the side door.

By now, however, no one wanted to step into that back alley. The way bullets were flying, it was just as scary for the hostages as for the robbers. Alex Spears had the misfortune of being the first person shoved out the side door, and was immediately stuck in the jaw by a bullet. Although bandits yelled for him to get in the car, he slipped around the corner, and hid in the dead-end alley behind the bank.

Left to right: Jewell Poe, Vance Littleton, Freda Stroebel (photo courtesy of Conrad Hilton Center)

Pandemonium ensued as more customers clumped out the door. Oscar Cliett followed soon after, and although a bullet clipped his heel, he also managed to escape.

Lewis Davis thought he could clear the way by firing a few shots to scare the crowd. Instead, the moment he stepped into the alley, bullets struck his side, neck, and both arms. The severely wounded Davis lurched his way into the back seat of the getaway car.

Jewell Poe made it out of the bank unscathed, as did

Freda Stroebel, who despite being used as a human shield, managed to twist away from Santa's grasp. Stroebel later admitted that in that moment, she feared the vigilantes more than the bandits because innocent bystanders were being struck by bullets.

As Stroebel and Poe glanced around for a safe hiding place, a dentist poked his head out a window above and advised them to dash into the "little alley" behind the bank. As the shootout continued, the bookkeepers lay flat on the ground and waited for it to end.

According to Stroebel, Poe was more frightened than she. "I would have been more scared," she explained later, "but I guess I was just dumb. I was calmer than Mr. Poe. He was nervous. He nearly died."

Friendly Fire

Marion Olson was the next to be struck by friendly fire, taking a bullet in the thigh. Although the robbers shoved Olson into the back seat of the car, the young man promptly slid out the other side and limped his way to freedom.

Like Olson, Brady Boggs and Pete Rutherford were also shot in the leg. Unlike Olson, these two were not even bank patrons. Boggs was struck in the leg while racing towards the scene to help, while Rutherford was half a block away when a stray bullet caught him in the thigh.

Cisco's trio of peace officers were among the few people with enough restraint to wait for a clear shot at an actual criminal before firing. Officer Bedford saw

From left to right: Cisco police chief, G.E. Bedford and Cisco deputy G.W. Carmichael (photos courtesy of the Conrad Hilton Center)

his chance as Freda Stroebel broke free from Santa, and immediately took aim.

Local Heroes Fall

Unfortunately, Bedford's new shotgun jammed as he stepped into the alley, and his large frame made a clear target. Even so, Bedford kept on walking towards the side door. He managed to get a few shots off before being struck five times in the torso. To the shock and horror of Cisco's citizens, their beloved police chief fell first to his knees, then flat on his back at the east end of the alley.

A little girl named Alice Spencer had the misfortune of witnessing Bedford's demise. At the time of the robbery, the 7-year-old and her mother were shopping at Garner's Department Store, right across the alley from the bank. Before entering the business, Alice saw her friend Frances Blasingame follow Santa into the First National Bank. While Mrs. Spencer agreed to visit Santa Claus, she insisted on completing their errands first.

A few minutes later, as Alice and her mother exited the store, they heard gunshots and shouting. Alice looked down the street and noticed Chief Bedford standing at the mouth of the alley with a gun in his hand. Mrs. Spencer pulled Alice into the family car, where they took cover as the gun battle raged. After several terrifying minutes, a man saw them cowering in the car, and using his body to protect them, he led the Spencers back into Garner's Department Store.

"I do not know who the man was," Alice Spencer later said, "but it was the bravest act I have ever seen in my life."

Once the gunfight ended, Alice and her mother saw Chief Bedford carried past the store window. "He was still alive," according to Alice. "Every time his heart would beat, blood would gush from the wounds in his chest. For a 7-year-old that was a frightening sight."

With Bedford down, Officer Carmichael stepped out from the dead end alley behind the bank. As with Bedford, Carmichael only managed to fire a few shots before being struck down, in his case, by a bullet through the brain.

Little Girls Nabbed by Bandits

A brief lull ensued, during which Santa tossed his sack into the back seat and climbed in beside the severely injured Davis. Helms ordered the two little girls to get in, but only Emma Mae Robinson complied. Laverne Comer tried to run away but reported that, "Santa jerked me by my wrist into the car."

From left to right: Marion Olson and Laverne Comer (photos courtesy of the Conrad Hilton Center)

Robert Hill and Vance Littleton were the last to emerge from the bank. The bandit used the bookkeeper as a human shield, and neither was injured. As Hill hopped into the driver's seat, Littleton escaped.

Cafe Owner Nearly Ends It

Before Hill could do anything about Littleton, a local café owner named R. L. Davis made a move that could have ended the caper right then and there; he charged towards the driver's side of the Buick, held a gun to Robert Hill's head, and fired – or at least he tried to. Although fully loaded, Day's weapon had been given to him at the hardware store and he did not know how to work the safety.

Day pulled the trigger twice and had his own scalp grazed by a stray bullet, before grumbling, "How do you work this durned thing, anyway?" As Hill frantically started the car, the gun finally went off, striking the side of Garner's Department Store rather than making Day's day.

When the getaway car reached the street, the bandits turned right onto Avenue D. Postal worker Will Coldwell, who had a reputation for outstanding marksmanship, put his service revolver to good use. "I fired five times," he later explained, "once at the gas tank and four at the left rear tire." Coldwell's tire shot caused the Buick to skid so violently that the back door opened and Emma Mae nearly flew off Santa's lap. Alex Spears, who had been watching from his hiding place, saw the two little girls and quickly warned Officer R. T. Redies and others about the young hostages in the getaway car.

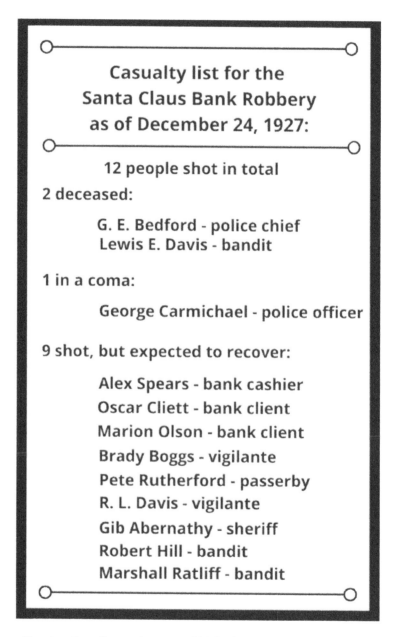

Here's a list of casualties as of 12/24/1927 © Tui Snider

Chapter 7
Messy Getaway

Foiled by a Teen

The bandits sped away with Hill at the wheel, Ratliff firing through a hole in the rear window, and Helms tossing out roofing nails to puncture pursuer's tires. Davis, meanwhile, was so injured he could barely sit up. The fancy blue Buick, however, was in worse shape than Davis. Hill struggled to steer the vehicle due to its flat tire, and it was nearly out of gas. None of them had thought to fill up after their long drive from Wichita Falls.

Meanwhile, the Harris family pulled into Cisco from the nearby town of Rising Star. They were ready for a day of Christmas shopping and completely unaware of the danger ahead. At the wheel sat 14-year-old Woodrow Wilson Harris, known as "Woody" to family and friends. Woody's 80-year-old grandmother sat beside him and his parents were in back. As the Harris family's Oldsmobile neared Fourteenth Street and Avenue D, a haggard Santa with a bloodstained beard flagged the car down.

After Hill fired a shot into the air, Helms

approached the front passenger window and told Woody's 80-year-old grandmother to leave. When she turned her head to ignore him, Helms opened the passenger door and yanked her out. At this, Woody's mother began screaming. Helms told her to shut up or he would shoot. Mrs. Harris stopped screaming, but only long enough to say she couldn't help it. She then began screaming again, while her husband assured Helms he would calm her down. Santa pointed a gun at Woodrow.

14-year-old Woodrow Wilson Harris a.k.a. "Woody" foiled an attempted carjacking by the Santa Claus bank robbers. (photo courtesy of the Conrad Hilton Center.)

"Get out," he said, "and make it damn quick."

"Yes, sir," Woody replied. "Wait until I throw it out of gear." He then cleverly locked the steering column and pocketed the car keys.

Hill Helps Woody's Grandmother

Meanwhile, Robert Hill quietly assisted Woody's grandmother and parents by walking them to a nearby house where they could take refuge. As Woody stood by the car trying to assess the situation, he noticed Laverne and Emma Mae huddled by the side of the road. He asked them what was going on, but the little girls were too terrified to reply.

With the bandits distracted by transferring provisions to the Oldsmobile, Woody made a run for it. Seeing this, Marshall Ratliff fired a couple of shots towards the boy.

Woody Takes Cover

As if that wasn't bad enough, the approaching posse mistook Woody for a fugitive, so they began firing at him, too. "Everyone from 10 to 60 was out there with a gun," Woody later recalled. "They thought *I* was a bank robber." Thankfully, Woody found cover in a shed before becoming another casualty.

As Santa and his gang situated themselves in the Harris family Oldsmobile, they discovered that Lewis Davis had lost consciousness and could not be roused. It wasn't easy, but they carried his limp body over to the Harris' car and propped him in the back seat next to the money bag. They grabbed the girls, hopped into the car, and were ready to go when Robert Hill realized what Woody Harris had done.

Forced to Change Cars

With the posse less than a block away, the bandits were forced to return to the beat up Buick. There was no time to grab Davis, so they left him behind. During this transition, Hill's left arm was struck by a high-powered rifle. The force of the bullet swung him completely around.

As the men pulled away, the posse descended on the Harris family's car. Inside they found the unconscious Davis, 2 pistols, 3 cartridge belts, and an Idaho Potato sack full of money. *However, in all the commotion, the men had forgotten their loot!*

Posse Retrieves the Loot

Although the bandits were gone by the time the posse arrived, they are thrilled to retrieve the loot. During the heist, Jewell Poe handed Santa $12,200 in cash along with $150,000 in non-negotiable securities. To everyone's surprise, not only was all the money accounted for, but according to Jewell Poe, the amount recovered was $4 over the pilfered amount!

Alex Spears decided to keep the bank open for the rest of the day rather than close early. Only then did he go to the hospital to have his gunshot wound treated.

As for Woody Harris, once he emerged from hiding

and his family vouched for his identity, the posse sent him on an unusual errand. They needed the young man to drive Lewis Davis to the hospital!

On Foot

While the posse dealt with the Harris' car, the robbers limped on in their bullet-riddled Buick with its flattened tires and nearly empty gas tank. After hearing Santa grumble about a gunshot wound to the chin, Laverne Comer turned around and glimpsed the face beneath his fake whiskers. She was caught in the act, however, and one of the men smacked her head with the butt of his gun.

About 5 miles from town, in an attempt to throw pursuers off track, the bandits turned onto an unpaved lane. With their gasoline dwindling, Hill finally abandoned the dirt road completely, driving into brush and trees until the car would go no further.

Girls Left Behind

As the three men grabbed their remaining supplies, they decided to leave Laverne and Emma Mae behind. They made the girls lie on the floor of the vehicle, warning them not to look or they would both be shot. Even so, as the men trudged off into the rugged terrain, Laverne bravely snuck a peek and noticed Santa was limping. It was a good thing the girls started yelling when police arrived a few minutes later because the posse nearly opened fire on the abandoned Buick before checking who was inside.

Laverne IDs Santa

The girls were mostly unscathed, although Laverne had a lump on her head from being whacked with the gun. It was worth it, however, because that glance combined with the familiar tone of his voice enabled the little girl to I.D. the man in the Santa Claus outfit. Laverne told police her mom had recently bought the Manhattan Café from Santa's Mom, a woman named Mrs. Carter. According to Laverne, the man in the Santa suit was Carter's son, Marshall Ratliff. From there, police swiftly connected the dots between Ratliff, Wichita Falls, and the men he boarded with at the Herron's house.

Chapter 8
Massive Manhunt for Santa

The Hunt for Santa's Gang

The site of the battered Buick served as a gathering place for the largest man hunt the state of Texas had ever seen. By late afternoon, some newspapers claim that over 1,000 men joined the search for the Santa Claus bank robber and his crew. In addition to law enforcement agents, the posse included hundreds of citizens fueled by sheer excitement and the possibility of getting a piece of the $5000 Dead Bank Robbers Reward.

With so many people involved, you would think Ratliff, Helms, and Hill would have been found in short order. Unfortunately, many searchers were more exuberant than organized. Each time a clue turned up, curious men rushed to look at the item rather than continue examining their designated area.

One of the first discoveries was Santa's discarded beard and bullet-riddled jacket. Other finds included a suitcase full of first aid supplies, cans of food, and Robert Hill's blood- stained overcoat, complete with a hole in the left sleeve where he'd been struck by a bullet. Unfortunately, by the time bloodhounds arrived, the trail was too scattered and trampled by horses for the dogs to follow.

MANY CITIZENS JOIN IN SEARCH FOR FOUR ROBBERS WHO MADE ESCAPE

They still weren't sure how many bandits they were pursuing. This headline mentions 4 robbers. (Corsicana Daily Sun, Dec 24, 1927)

Famous Penpals Discuss the Manhunt

In a letter to fellow writer H.P. Lovecraft, Texas author Robert E. Howard (creator of Conan the Barbarian) explained that he and his friends were too hung over to take part in the search for Santa Claus:

"When we went to the town, we found the countryside in an uproar; for while we lay drunk, the 'Santa Claus' gang that had looted Southwestern banks for more than a year, had swept into Cisco, 35 miles away and in an attempt to rob the main bank, had raved into a wholesale gun- battle that strewed the streets with dead and wounded," he wrote. "Two or three of them had gotten away into the brush and posses were beating the hills for them. To invitations to join the man-hunt, my friends and I laughed hollowly; we were in no shape to even lift a gun to our shoulders, much less confront a band of desperate outlaws."

Police Find Clews to Yeggs Sought In Texas

Bloody Cotton and Rags Indicate One Is Badly Wounded.

A taste of 1920s slang: "Yeggs" are "bank robbers" (Louisville Courier-Journal, Dec 25, 1927)

Blue Norther Dampens Vigilantes' Spirits

Shortly after sunset, one of the Lone Star State's sudden cold fronts a.k.a. "a blue norther" swept in, taking much of the manhunt's merriment with it. As temperatures dropped and sleet fell, the search party dwindled in size, leaving only peace officers and the most diligent citizens.

Another Injury

William Gilbert "Gib" Abernathy was one of eight sheriffs involved in that initial manhunt, even though December 23, 1927 marked his 27th wedding anniversary. Unfortunately for Abernathy, his rifle accidentally discharged during the search, blowing off a couple fingers and severing an artery in his right leg.

Although he required several blood transfusions, Abernathy survived and went on to become a Texas Ranger. You can bet that was one wedding anniversary he never forgot!

Chapter 9
The Mysterious Blonde

Chief Bedford's Startling Claim

From his hospital bed in Cisco, Chief Bedford made a startling claim. "It wasn't a man who shot me," he insisted. "It was a blonde-headed woman. I was looking her straight in the eyes when she fired." Even after Cisco's mayor, J.M. Williamson, released a statement that no women were involved in the bank robbery, Bedford's mysterious blonde crept into a few news reports.

Despite Bedford's insistence, as far as anyone could recall, the only females at the bank that day were Freda Stroebel and the two little girls, all brunettes. When I first heard Bedford's claim, I thought he may have mistaken Santa's white beard for blonde hair. As my research continued, however, I began to take Bedford's claims seriously. Sadly, Bedford never got a chance to explain himself in more detail. Cisco's beloved police chief passed away at 7:45 p.m. Friday evening.

After Bedford's death, the crowd that had slowly gathered outside the hospital began to worry local peace officers. To avoid a possible mob lynching, officials quietly transferred Lewis Davis to Fort Worth. Davis, who was in and out of consciousness, was so bleary that his interrogation was nearly worthless.

Davis eventually told cops his real name, but the names he gave for his companions turned out to be prominent business men of Wichita Falls rather than his own motley crew.

Woman Sought In Cisco Killing

Austin American Statesman, Dec 29, 1927

Somber Christmas

As the manhunt combed the countryside south of Cisco, the bandits turned north. After all the commotion at the bank, no one expected them to return to town, but that's exactly what they did. Ratliff didn't want to be recognized, so he waited in a secluded area while Helms and Hill prowled Cisco's neighborhoods to steal a car.

Late Friday night, the men made off with a Model T Ford they nabbed a mere block away from the First National Bank. After picking up Ratliff, the men headed west for a few hours before pulling into a

CISCO POLICE CHIEF KILLED BY BANDITS; POSSE IN PURSUIT

Victoria Advocate, Dec 25, 1927

wooded area to sleep. Although it was an open-air touring car and the night had turned chilly, the bank robbers did not dare light a fire.

Quick Stop at the Ranch

Exhausted and weak from injuries, the men slept through the daylight hours of Saturday, December 24. That evening, they took back roads and made it to the Fox ranch near Moran around 2:00 a.m.

Minnie Fox answered the door this time. She brewed the men coffee and fed them chicken, dressing, and cake she had prepared for her family's Christmas Eve meal.

Minnie also dressed the men's wounds, although Ratliff refused to have the bullet in his leg taken out. He said it wasn't bothering him so they ought to leave it alone. Ratliff spent much of his time slouched in a chair with his hat pulled low, scouring the newspaper account of the robbery to see how much police knew.

Bad News

Minnie confirmed what the men suspected; her brother, Lewis, had died from his injuries on the night of the bank robbery. After a neighbor alerted her to his condition, Minnie raced into Cisco to visit him. Unfortunately, by the time she got to the hospital, her brother had already been transferred to Fort Worth.

Somber Christmas for Cisco

It was a somber Christmas throughout the region. With Chief Bedford dead, Deputy Carmichael in a coma, and many others injured or just plain traumatized, the mood slipped from festive to morose as swiftly as the weather had slipped from sun to sleet.

Whether true or not, one widely circulated anecdote sums it up best. At a church in nearby Eastland the story goes, when a man dressed as St. Nick entered the congregation during a Christmas Eve service, a sobbing little boy called out, "Santa Claus, why did you rob that bank?"

Chapter 10
A Close Call

Henry Helms' Request

Although grateful for Minnie's assistance, the bandits did not want to put the Fox family in any more danger than they already had, so they left after a couple of hours. This ended up being a wise move for them.

Remember the unusual request Henry Helms made of his landlady on the night he and his gang left Wichita Falls? Helms asked Josephine Herron to send Dr. J.T. Vick down to the Fox family ranch if he and the boys ran into trouble.

It's still unclear exactly how Josephine knew that her boarders were in trouble. Maybe she simply read the newspapers and put two and two together. In any case, on the evening of Sunday, December 25, 1927 Mrs. Josephine Herron, Dr. J.T. Vick, and his housekeeper, Essie Thornton, drove from Wichita Falls to the Fox family ranch. It's worth noting that Dr. Vick and Mrs. Thornton, a widower, were later married, although some newspapers initially refer to her as "Mrs. Murphy." A pseudonym, perhaps?

What the trio didn't know is that by the time they

got to the Fox ranch it was under police surveillance. When the travelers arrived, they were promptly arrested. If only the police had arrived earlier, they might have caught the bandits and ended our story right there.

Some researchers speculate that Josephine Herron was already at the Fox residence when Dr. Vick and his companion arrived, and that she merely pretended to have ridden down with them to avoid being linked to the Cisco robbery. I think this is worth considering.

Corsicana Daily Sun, Dec 28, 1927

Eight People Arrested and Questioned

The next day, several mourners were taken into custody at the conclusion of Lewis Davis' funeral in Wichita Falls. The police now had eight persons of interest in jail, including: Dr. Vick, Mrs. Thornton, Josephine Herron, Sam Fox, Minnie Fox, and three of their grown children, who were visiting for the holidays.

After questioning them individually, all were

released - with one exception. Can you guess who?

When questioned by police Minnie Fox came clean immediately, admitting that she had fed and nursed the bandits the night before. In her defense, she merely stated that while she did not condone their behavior, taking care of them seemed "the decent thing to do." She was eventually released along with everyone except for Mrs. Josephine Herron.

Unlike the rest, Mrs. Herron was eventually charged with being an accessory to murder after the fact. Of course, as you may have already guessed, A.C. Greene glosses over this part. Yes, he mentions everyone who was arrested, but he fails to mention the charges placed against Mrs. Herron.

Anonymous Tipster Mentions Blonde

Around the time of these arrests, the Wichita Falls police department received tips from an anonymous source claiming that a blonde woman wearing military garb was involved in robbing Cisco's First National Bank. It's interesting to note that upon her arrest, newspapers referred to Josephine Herron's "mannish attire" which included a khaki shirt and trousers along with rugged mid-calf workboots that she called "bootees."

Newspapers also mention that her reddish brown hair "looked as if it were dyed." Could Josephine Herron be the mysterious blonde-headed woman wearing military garb who some witnesses claim to have seen at the robbery?

One Held Now.

Sheriff Bralley was attempting to
account for movements last Friday
of a Wichita Falls woman with
dyed hair. The woman is being
held in jail at Albany under a
charge of accessory to murder after
the fact.

Austin American Statesman, Dec 29, 1927

Mannish Attire, Military Garb & Dyed Hair

While Dr. Vick and Essie Thornton were not quoted in any articles I could find, Josephine Herron had a lot to say. The impression she made on one reporter was a mixed bag. While the article first says Mrs. Herron, "displayed a keen wit and her dark eyes flashed while she talked," it soon adds that, "Her talk was somewhat illiterate at times."

While in custody, Josephine Herron admitted that she had made the Santa outfit and purchased the Santa mask that Ratliff wore during the Cisco holdup.

She also told police that in addition to robbing banks and stealing cars, Henry Helms, "operated a 'dope line' from El Paso to Tulsa, Oklahoma and had told her the names of numerous physicians to whom he sold smuggled narcotics."

Reading all these newspaper accounts really makes me wonder just how involved in this whole escapade was she? When Mrs. Blasingame alerted Cisco police to the crime in progress, she stated that as many as eight bandits were involved. Was that first shot fired through the bank window meant to alert Josephine Herron and/or other accomplices?

ACTIVITIES OF GANG TOLD BY MRS. HERRON

Abilene Reporter-News, Jan 1, 1928

My Missed Opportunity

While visiting the Lela Latch Lloyd Museum in Cisco, I met a lifelong resident who told me his grandfather recalled seeing a "blonde-headed woman driving a car" on the outskirts of town shortly after the robbery, and he thought "she was there to meet the men." At the time of our chat, I wasn't yet taking the blonde-headed woman seriously. I kick myself to this day for not writing down that gentleman's name.

And while the Santa Claus bank robbery is often presented as if the Valera hold-up was the only other heist Marshall Ratliff ever committed, newspapers of the time make it clear that many people suspected his involvement in several other robberies as part of a gang led by Henry Helms.

WOMAN QUIZZED IN BANK HOLDUP

Texas Matron Admits Nursing Bandits; Bonds Found in Her Home.

The matron mentioned in the headline is Josephine Herron. (Lincoln Star, Jan 1, 1928)

Possible Links to Other Bank Robberies

Someone who believed the Helms' gang was involved in multiple holdups was Wichita County Sheriff W.G. Brailey. Brailey also took Bedford's blonde-headed woman very seriously, especially after the same tipster helped police recover stolen loot from a bank robbery in Bangs, a little town about 60 miles south of Cisco.

This particular bank robbery happened on November 9, 1927, which, incidentally, is the same day the Texas State Bank Association upped its robber bounty to $5,000. According to the informant, a fruit jar with Liberty bonds was buried in Wichita Falls.

WOMAN ADMITS MAKING SUITS FOR BANDITS

Says Work Was Done Without Knowledge of Purpose of Gang.

Austin American Statesman, Dec 31, 1927

Stolen Loot Found at the Herron Home

Sure enough, Sheriff Brailey and his men discovered a fruit jar containing $1.3 million in Liberty bonds right where the tipster said it would be – in the Herron family's backyard! Shortly after, a bank cashier from Bangs identified the bonds as part of the funds stolen in their recent robbery.

Was Josephine Herron aware of any of these activities? Was she an accomplice to the gangsters or was she simply a good-hearted woman who was oblivious to their crimes?

Feverish Delusions or Something Else?

As you can see, Sheriff Brailey's reasons for believing in the mysterious blonde-headed were based on fact, not fancy. Could Josephine Herron be the mysterious blonde-headed woman so many people, including myself, have dismissed as a dying man's feverish delusions?

Chapter 11
Desperate Measures

Kidnapping and Carjacking

The three fugitives, of course, were oblivious to their close call at the Fox ranch and the subsequent arrests of their friends and family. At sunrise, they once again found a secluded area to sleep for the day. It was Christmas, and one can imagine it must have been a lonely holiday full of regrets for the bandit trio as they shivered in their open vehicle, too afraid to light a fire.

At sunset, the men hit the road again, with Henry Helms at the wheel this time. The gunshot wound in Robert Hill's arm made him too sore to drive. A few hours into their back road trek, Helms struck a cattle guard and planted the car in a ditch near the Wylie family's farm.

Stories here vary considerably, but according to Carl Wylie, "The robbers came to our place soon after midnight Sunday, saying they had a sick man and wanted to borrow a car. My father told them I was away but would return soon."

Since the Wylie family did not own a phone, the 21-

year-old's dad, Mr. R.C. Wylie, couldn't call a doctor for the men. Up until that moment, Mr. Wylie didn't see much use for modern contraptions like the telephone. He thought it promoted idle gossip. Although word of the robbery had yet to reach the Wylie farm, something about the men made Mr. Wylie uneasy. He kept his shotgun handy, just in case.

Marshall News Messenger, Dec 27, 1927

More Friendly Fire

Mr. Wylie's instincts were correct. When Carl arrived, the bandits pulled guns on him, hopped in the car, and told his son to drive off. As the men sped away, Mr. Wylie fired at the car. The only one struck, however, was his son. Fortunately, Carl's wounds were minor.

This put Carl Wylie in a tricky situation. If he ran

away, his kidnappers would shoot him. He might also be shot if police or vigilantes took up the chase, especially if they had visions of collecting the Dead Bank Robbers Reward. How could pursuers tell Carl from his kidnappers, especially with him at the wheel?

Youth Not Shot
By Bank Bandits

Oops! Carl's dad accidentally shot his son during his kidnapping. (Corsicana Daily Sun, Dec 27, 1927)

Carl decided to play along as best as he could, driving the back roads, avoiding oncoming cars, siphoning gas, and shivering through the night without a fire to keep warm. To make things worse, the robbers were low on provisions. They only had two oranges, which they did not share with Carl. One of them even stole his overcoat.

A little over 24 hours into Carl Wylie's kidnapping, the group pulled into the outskirts of Breckenridge, a small town roughly 30 miles north of Cisco. It was here that, "One of the robbers scouted around until he found a Ford touring car without curtains," according to Carl.

After a terse discussion, the bandits took off in their

newly stolen car, leaving Carl alone in his own.

"We could take you out and tie you and gag you – or kill you," they warned Carl. "But we are letting you off light." Before departing, the gangsters took a moment to shake Carl's hand and wish him luck.

Once Carl drove into town he discovered it was actually Cisco, not Breckenridge as they mistakenly thought. All that backroad meandering in the middle of the night had mixed them up. So at 5:00 a.m. on Tuesday, December 27, 1927, Carl Wylie found his way to the Cisco Police Department to report his kidnapping.

You've got to wonder if this incident changed Mr. Wylie's attitude towards telephones.

Chapter 12
Trail of Blood

Santa Meets Old Betsy

With no back seat, their latest stolen car, a 1924 Model T roadster, made a snug fit for the three men. They were in no position to complain, however. Frantic and hungry, the bandits headed north out of Cisco, planning to cross the Brazos River near the town of South Bend, roughly 50 miles away.

Meanwhile, in South Bend another big posse of officers and citizen volunteers set up a road block. Those in attendance included the legendary Texas Rangers, Captain Tom Hickman and Manuel Trazazas "Lone Wolf" Gonzaullas, who had a high powered machine gun in their car.

The bank robbers nearly drove straight into the road block. According to Robert Hill, "We didn't see the officers until we got right at South Bend about a block from them." Panicked, the men turned around. When the posse caught sight of the armed men in their open-seated roadster, it kicked off another car chase and shootout.

Once again, the pursuers took aim at the getaway car's tires. Soon, one was not only flattened, but the tire completely peeled off, leaving only a rim. Helms struggled to control the vehicle and was forced to slow down. As the posse gained ground, the robbers abandoned the roadster and tried to hide in the brush near some oil wells.

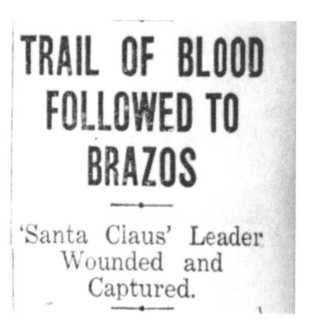

TRAIL OF BLOOD FOLLOWED TO BRAZOS

'Santa Claus' Leader Wounded and Captured.

Austin American Statesman, Dec 27, 1927

By now, Ratliff was in such bad shape he could barely walk. Deputy Silas "Si" Bradford aimed for him first, using Old Betsy, his trusty shot gun, to take down Santa with a single blast. Bradford's shotgun also struck Helms and Hill, but they managed to escape.

Upon Marshall Ratliff's capture, officers discovered three ammo belts, six hand guns, a double-barreled

Wounded and Hungry Pair Run Down at Graham.

Austin American Statesman, Dec 30, 1927

shotgun, and a bowie knife on his body. He had six bullet wounds, too, and was in such bad shape they thought he might die.

Ratliff remained unconscious, or at least feigning it, as officers sent him to a hospital in Graham. They could not identify him immediately, but several clues led them to suspect they had Cisco's Santa Claus bandit. For starters, his suit contained a label from a Wichita Falls laundry, and his cap had a label from a clothing store there. Ratliff's bullet wounds included one in his jaw, and they knew from little Laverne Comer and other eyewitnesses that Santa had a bloody chin.

When R.L. Wilson, Cisco's nighttime police chief, arrived in Graham, he made the final I.D. saying, "That is Marshall Ratliff. I have known him for many years." Wilson also remarked that although Ratliff was a natural blond, his hair was now dyed black.

With Ratliff tucked away, two bandits remained at large. Texas Ranger Captain Tom Hickman

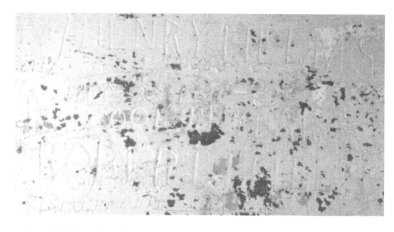

The Old Eastland County Jail cell still bears the inscription: "Henry Helms, Robert Hill, Dec 23, 1927, Cool 99 years, Cisco bandits" on the wall. (photo taken by the author)

commanded a posse on the ground, while Lone Wolf Gonzaullas took to the sky in a government-owned biplane armed with a machine gun. Although the fugitives were sighted several times, capturing them was not an easy feat.

Robert Hill later remarked, "We run down [to] the Brazos River and got under a rock finally, and we stayed there all day." Although they managed to evade another large manhunt over the next 2 days, the men had nothing to eat or drink and were in bad shape. Old Betsy had done a lot of damage, and the men grew weaker by the minute. Of the two, Henry Helms was in the worst. His infected wounds had triggered a high fever and chills.

Finally, on Thursday night, the two men staggered into the town of Graham where they snagged a couple ears of corn and took shelter in a barn. Early Friday morning, the pair wandered into the Texan Hotel. Helms was too delirious to speak, so Hill asked the desk clerk if a Mr. Fields was around. As the clerk told them no, he glimpsed a cartridge belt on one of the men. Suspecting their true identities, he called the sheriff's department the moment they left.

As cops cruised the streets of Graham it didn't take them long to find the two fugitives. Helms was in such a weakened state that he gave up without resistance. Hill, however, made a feeble attempt to run. "I figured we were going to be killed anyhow," he explained later, "on account of the bank reward, and I figured it was just as well to get killed running as with our hands up."

Another Shotgun Injury

Shortly after the men's capture, the Santa Claus manhunt suffered another casualty as Young County Judge W.F. Parsley's shotgun accidentally fired as he unloaded it. Parsley survived, but his foot required amputation. On a grimmer note, Cisco's Deputy George Carmichael passed away on January 7, 1928 from the bullet wound he received during the bank robbery.

Ratliff and Helms were briefly held in Graham before being transferred to Eastland County Jail where Ratliff was already in custody. If you look closely at the photo above, you can see the graffiti that the men inscribed in their jail cell while they were held there.

While some newspapers reported that Helms was at

death's door and not expected to pull through, both he and Ratliff eventually recovered from their wounds. At first, however, Ratliff seemed unable to talk due to his injured jaw, although jailers claimed he spoke just fine in his sleep.

Crowd at Hill and Helms' capture. (photo courtesy of the Conrad Hilton Center)

Close up: Hill on the left, Helms on the right, with his eyes down. (photo courtesy of the Conrad Hilton Center)

Chapter 13
The Bandits Go to Court

Marshall Ratliff's First Trial

On January 23, 1928, Marshall Ratliff stood trial for his role in the Santa Claus bank robbery. In what the *Corsicana Daily Sun* described as "one of the most spectacular trials in the history of the 91st District," Ratliff pled not-guilty to robbing Cisco's First National Bank.

When Laverne Comer took the stand, she was unable to recognize Marshall Ratliff. Considering she had ID'd him during the getaway and later tipped off police, this came as quite a surprise. Emma Mae Robinson made up for it by pointing straight at Marshall Ratliff when her turn came.

Traumatized Child

Laverne later lamented that she attended court so often in 1928 that she flunked 7th grade. Decades later, she told an interviewer she still had nightmares about the event, and not just during the holidays. These days, we would probably say she had PTSD and get her some therapy.

Ratliff Attempt To Escape Jail Is Nipped by Sheriff

Henry Helms Confined In Same Cell Where Bar Found Loose.

Austin American Statesman, Jan 26, 1928

Attempted Jailbreak

Even though the prosecution had over 50 people willing to testify and the defense had none, Ratliff remained upbeat throughout his four-day trial.

A couple days into the proceedings, jailers detected a loose panel along with a hidden iron bar in the cell Ratliff shared with Henry Helms and another prisoner. Perhaps part of his smug court demeanor was fueled by the idea that he and Helms thought they would be escaping.

With jailers vowing to keep a closer eye on the Santa Claus bandits, the trial resumed. And while the prosecution easily proved that Ratliff was present at the Cisco crime scene, none of its witnesses could remember actually seeing him fire his gun.

Devoted Mother

Throughout it all, Rilla Carter gave her son all the support she could muster. After his capture, she attended to his wounds in jail. When his trial began, she was the first to arrive and the last to leave the courtroom each day. Mrs. Carter also took notes during proceedings and spoke often with her son's court-appointed legal counselor.

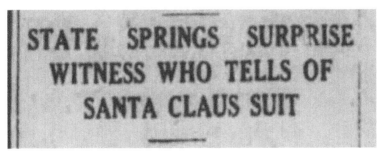

Josephine Herron's daughter was a surprise witness
(Corsicana Daily Sun, Jan 25, 1928)

Surprise Witness

Another surprise during Marshall Ratliff's first trial occurred when Josephine Herron's daughter, Marion, was called to the stand as a surprise witness. By testifying, the 15-year-old hoped to help her mother, who was charged with being an accessory after the fact to murder. Perhaps it did, because all charges were eventually dropped against Mrs. Herron. (Although A.C. Greene mentions Marion testifying, he uses a pseudonym for her and fails to mention the charges against her mother.)

On January 27, 1928, Ratliff was convicted of armed robbery and sentenced to 99 years in prison. If the verdict upset him, Ratliff did not let it show. As he left the courtroom, Ratliff made it known that he viewed this lengthy sentence as little more than a minor inconvenience by saying, "That's no hill for a high stepper like me."

"THEY POURED IT ON ME," ONLY COMMENT OF EAST-LAND BANDIT

Amarillo Globe-Times, Feb 27, 1928

Henry Helms' Trial

On February 20, 1928 Henry Helms went to trial for his part in robbing Cisco's First National Bank. Since Marshall Ratliff had received a 99-year sentence rather than the death penalty, Helms told a family member he felt optimistic.

Bandit Tells Jury Of His Childhood

Hill Relates Story Of Hardship.

Austin American Statesman, Mar 23, 1928

Despite the presence of his pregnant wife, Nettie, and their five young children, Helms did not come across as a loving family man during the trial. Lacking Ratliff's jaunty air, Helms was a brooding figure who kept his head down and rarely spoke. If anything, onlookers pitied Nettie Helms and her children instead of feeling sympathy for Henry Helms.

Like Ratliff, Helms pled not guilty while having no witnesses for his defense, and more than enough willing to testify against him. Several witnesses, including Alex Spears, described Helms firing pistols from the bank's side door, while Freda Stroebel mentioned his angry tone when he caught her looking at him. Even Carl Wylie recalled Helms saying he was ready for another shootout if the situation called for it.

Henry Helms received the death sentence for his part in the bank robbery on February 26, 1928. As his wife sobbed from her seat in the courtroom, Helms is said to have remarked, "Well, they poured it on me."

Robert Hill: The Boy Who Never had a Chance

At his trial on March 19, 1928, Robert Hill was neither as upbeat and nattily attired as Marshall Ratliff, nor as glowering and aloof as Henry Helms. Of the three, Robert Hill expressed the most remorse. For one thing, Hill signed a confession admitting his role in the Cisco bank robbery shortly, while the other two pled not guilty.

Throughout the trial, Hill's court-appointed lawyer referred to him as, "the boy who never had a chance." The defense carefully recounted Robert Hill's upbringing and how the odds were stacked against him, providing witnesses to back up this character profile. According to Hill's defense, the state of Texas was to blame for sending this orphaned boy to a reformatory rather than a foster home where he might have had better role models in life.

Finally, Hill took the stand and poured his heart out to the crowded courtroom. He made it clear that while he had fired his guns, he never aimed directly at anyone. Hill admitted to firing four warning shots into the ceiling of the bank, and a couple more shots when carjacking the Harris family's Oldsmobile.

Hill also stressed, and witnesses confirmed, that he was the last man to leave the bank after the robbery. Since both Chief Bedford and Deputy Carmichael had been struck down by that time, this little detail instantly cleared Hill of their murders.

Hill Must Serve 99 Years for Part In Cisco Robbery

Longview News-Journal, Mar 26, 1928

As the jury deliberated, Hill openly fretted with those waiting in court with him, including a woman writing a book about the death penalty. Hill told her he was against execution, "Because it causes criminals like me to kill people. A man who thinks he is going to get the electric chair anyway thinks he might just as well fight it out."

Hill also spoke out against the $5,000 bounty for dead bank robbers, complaining that it made cops, "try to shoot us instead of catch us."

It only took the jury 40 minutes to reach a decision regarding Robert Hill. Like Marshall Ratliff, he was sentenced to 99 years in jail. Hill's reaction was one of great relief, and he later remarked how happy he was to have gotten his "two nines" instead of the death penalty.

Santa's Second Trial

Not only was March 26, 1928 Marshall Ratliff's 25th birthday, it was also the first day of his trial for the murders of Chief Bedford and Deputy George

Carmichael. This time, Marshall's defense had a witness – his devoted mother, Rilla Carter. Because of this, Mrs. Carter was not allowed inside the courtroom, so she diligently waited in the hallway during proceedings.

Like his first trial, this one also lasted 4 days, and Ratliff, sporting a new haircut and snappy bow tie, was cheery as ever. Despite all this, and while no one could testify to seeing him shoot a gun during the heist, on March 30, 1928 Marshall Ratliff was found guilty of murder. In addition to the death sentence, 198 years in prison were also assessed against him.

Both Ratliff and Helms appealed their death sentences. Both were denied, and shortly after, the two men were sent to the Texas State Prison in Huntsville to wait their turn on Death Row.

PRISON GATES CLOSE BANDIT CASE CHAPTER

Marshall Ratliff Taken To Huntsville Early Saturday By Officers

Abilene Reporter-News, Apr 29, 1928

Chapter 14
Desperation on Death Row

More Humane Than Hanging?

Although devised by Thomas Edison as a means to discredit rival inventor, Nikola Tesla, by graphically illustrating the dangers of alternating current, in the 1920s, the electric chair represented something entirely different to the public: Progress.

It was the dawning of the "Electric Age," after all, and this newly harnessed power transformed how Americans lived. Since legal executions often degenerated into macabre public spectacles, many argued that hanging was inhumane no matter how it was carried out. Electrocution, on the other hand, was seen as a more benevolent form of execution. Just flip a switch and the deed was done.

In 1923, Texas revised its criminal code for the execution process. Prior to that, inmates who received the death penalty were hanged, with executions taking place at the nearest county seat. From 1924 onward, executions were carried out at the Texas State Penitentiary in Huntsville, and prisoners were electrocuted.

Executions were a private affair, with a limited number of witnesses. The condemned even had a say regarding whether or not the press or family could attend. In these ways, the electric chair created a more discernible difference between legal execution and mob violence in the public's mind.

ELECTRIC CHAIR MAY REPLACE NOOSE IN TEXAS

El Paso Herald, Feb 8, 1923

Not Without Controversy

This new outlook was not without controversy in Texas. In 1924, the Huntsville warden, Mr. R.F. Coleman, was so upset by the new device that he resigned.

"A warden can't be a warden and a killer too," according to Coleman. "The penitentiary is a place to reform a man, not to kill him."

His replacement, Walter Monroe Miller, didn't mind a bit. "I have hanged several men while I was sheriff," he said, "and to touch the button or pull the switch means no more to me than pulling the lever on the gallows. At any rate it's more humane—the chair."

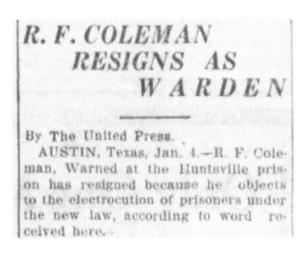

R. F. COLEMAN RESIGNS AS WARDEN

By The United Press.

AUSTIN, Texas, Jan. 4.—R. F. Coleman, Warned at the Huntsville prison has resigned because he objects to the electrocution of prisoners under the new law, according to word received here.

Taylor Daily Press, Jan 4, 1924

When the Roll is Called Up Yonder

In 1928, Death Row was a one story cinder block building with nine cells in a single row. Old Sparky, as the electric chair was often called, sat behind a green door at the hallway's end. Typically, the cell next to the green door was kept empty until execution day, when the condemned man was moved there for his final hours. As if playing a grim game of musical chairs, after each execution, the men advanced to the next cell, one step closer to their final destination.

Rilla Carter made the 300-mile trek to Huntsville as often as she could. Men on Death Row were allowed a few minor luxuries, so Rilla gave Marshall a wind-up phonograph and a few records, mostly hymns.

Marshall's mom was highly religious and hoped to convert her son before he met his maker.

Whether or not she succeeded, her gift prompted Marshall to start his own Death Row tradition, one that was widely reported in the newspapers. In those days, executions took place at midnight, and as the condemned man made his somber march towards the green door, Marshall would play "When the Roll is Called Up Yonder" on his gramophone.

Despite their proximity to Old Sparky, nearly a year passed before an execution date was set for Henry Helms or Marshall Ratliff. In the spring of 1929, Helms finally learned his official date with Old Sparky, September 6, 1929.

No mention was made of Ratliff's execution date. So in a letter to his sister, Effie, the ever- optimistic Ratliff expressed hopes that his own death sentence would be commuted.

WALKS TO EXECUTION ROOM TO TUNE "WHEN THE ROLL IS CALLED UP YONDER"

Corsicana Daily Sun, May 24, 1929

Hurry Up and Go Crazy!

Meanwhile, rumors swept through Death Row after a newcomer named Harry Leahy was whisked away when his attorney discovered a little-known Texas statute forbidding the execution of the insane. It didn't matter if a person was sane at the time of the crime, all that mattered was his mental state at death.

After learning of this loophole, Leahy quit eating. He started babbling, and acting strange. In response, Leahy's family and friends created a petition describing his feeble mental state, and he was granted a sanity hearing.

Leahy's loophole gave the inhabitants of Death Row a glimmer of hope, and they followed his case as closely as they could. Leahy's sanity hearing was unsuccessful, however. He was returned to Death Row and sent to Old Sparky shortly after.

Upon Leahy's return, he was quizzed by other prisoners as to why his insanity plea failed. "I just couldn't act the part," Leahy reportedly claimed. "They finally got to me. I couldn't keep going."

Henry Helms Goes Insane

"Well, watch me put it over," Helms allegedly replied. Despite this boast, it was already August. So, with September 6 right around the corner, Henry Helms went crazy as fast as he could. He stopped shaving, refused haircuts, and neglected to bathe. He shredded any paper he could find, including the Bible his wife had given him. He began staring oddly at the guards and muttering in a sing-song way.

Prison officials suspected a ruse, but admitted that the sing-song chanting continued even when Helms did not know they were near. His most common refrain went, "I ain't gonna sing no more, no more," which he would repeat a few times before calling out, "Hey!" or "Aye, aye, captain." Henry's family filed an appeal under the sanity statute, and in late August, Helms transferred to Eastland for a sanity hearing.

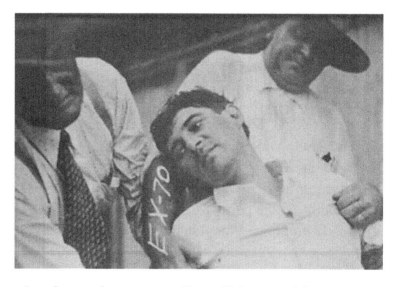

It took several men to move Henry Helms to and from court during his insanity hearing. (photo courtesy of the Conrad Hilton Center.)

Helms' Shocking Appearance

When Helms first appeared in court, onlookers were shocked by his vacant eyes, wild hair, and incessant

HELMS' WIFE TESTIFIES HUSBAND INSANE

Vernon Daily Record, Aug 30, 1929

sing-song chant. It took four men to lead Helms in and out of court because he struggled wildly when moved. Once seated, Helms rocked back and forth and muttered in a deep monotone. Some onlookers found his behavior so unsettling they fled the courtroom. A few women even excused themselves to vomit.

Helms seemed oblivious to the courtroom and frequently interrupted proceedings with shouts of, "Hey!" and "Aye, aye, captain!" He continued ripping paper, too, including legal documentation from his own lawyer.

Judge Davenport could not control Henry Helms' outbursts in court, but he did order a shave and a haircut for Helms. These tasks required four deputies, because Helms struggled and fought. Even so, on the third day of his trial, Helms arrived in court with a fresh look and clean clothes.

Family Testified that Helms was Insane

Judge Davenport gave the prosecution and defense 90 minutes each to present their cases. Witnesses for the defense included his parents, who described Henry's "peculiar traits from infancy." His wife, Nettie, also took the stand, describing how Helms was usually a devoted husband and father, but would occasionally disappear for days. An alienist, as psychiatrists were sometimes called, hired by the defense declared that Henry Helms was not of sound mind, even though his insanity had come on suddenly.

Another witness called by the defense was a Mr. Howard R. Whiteside, "who described himself as an itinerant student of the human mind." Despite these vague credentials, "The state offered no objection to his testimony and the court permitted his testimony to the effect that Helms was insane."

During Helms sanity hearing, it also came to light that shortly after his capture in Graham, he arranged for two of his .45 caliber pistols to be taken from evidence and sold to Texas Ranger Captain Tom Hickman. Hickman testified that he gave a Dallas jailer $25 for the guns, with the understanding that Henry's wife and kids would receive his payment. According to Nettie Helms, however, she never saw a penny.

ALIENISTS FOR BOTH SIDES EXAMINE CONDEMNED MAN IN CELL THURSDAY

Psychiatrists were often called "alienists" in the 1920s.
(Corsicana Semi-Weekly Light, Aug 30, 1929)

Avalanche of Opinion

Despite all the testimony for his insanity, witnesses for the state presented "an avalanche of opinion" to the contrary. Witnesses for the prosecution included a Texas Ranger, three jailers, and the superintendents from four state hospitals. In particular, the jailers noted that Helms had leadership qualities and was often the judge of the inmates' "kangaroo courts" while incarcerated.

And while it was later stricken from the record, the alleged conversation between Harry Leahy and Henry Helms in which Helms claimed he could do a better job of acting crazy was also mentioned in court as further evidence of his sanity.

Even Helms' lack of bad breath entered the debate, when Dr. T.B. Bass of the Abilene State Hospital cast his doubts due to the suddenness of Helms' insanity. According to Dr. Bass, "There is not the foul odor about the mouth which comes with swift and acute mania."

Jury's Decision in Ten Minutes Flat

After hearing both sides of the testimony, the jury took a mere 10 minutes to reach its decision; Henry Helms was declared to be of sound mind. While Helms appeared unaffected by the verdict, his mother "became hysterical" and a female spectator fainted. Henry, who was seated between his parents, merely continued to shred paper and mutter.

Upon his return to Huntsville, Henry Helms' cell was now the closest to the Green Door. As the countdown to his execution marched on, he continued to pace his cell while gripping a photo of his wife and children — and, of course, droning on in that strange sing-song voice.

In a touching gesture, the prisoners of Huntsville, many of whom truly believed Helms had gone crazy, pooled their funds to help him out. Together they scraped up $150 so Nettie Helms and her six children could take a train from her new home in New Mexico to the meet with the governer and ask for clemency on Helms' behalf. (You may recall that Nettie had five children when Helms originally went to trial; she was pregnant then with the sixth.)

If Ma Ferguson had still been governor, things may have gone differently. Ferguson disliked executions, and did everything in her power to forestall them. Even the current governor, Dan Moody, while not nearly as softhearted as Ferguson, often granted at least one 30-day stay of execution to those facing the death penalty. Unfortunately for the Helms family, in

Convicts Quick in Acts to Help Mate of Convicted Man

Rail Trip Fund Subscribed at Huntsville for Wife of Henry Helms

McAllen Daily Press, Aug 21, 1929

light of his insanity ruse, Governor Moody denied Helms a stay of execution.

On September 5th, 1929 Henry Helms received one final visit from his wife, 13-month-old daughter, and his parents. The last meal he chose was cabbage, sausages, tomatoes, and pie.

Final Gesture for a Condemned Friend

In his final moments, Henry Helms' fighting spirit kicked in one last time. It took four guards to drag him through the Green Door and strap him into Old Sparky.

Sadly, since Helms' family had spent so much money on his defense and travel, they were unable to retrieve his body after his execution. That's why he is buried at the Captain Joe Byrd Cemetery on prison grounds, or as the inmates called it, Peckerwood Hill.

Helms was executed shortly after midnight, but for the first time, perhaps in deference to his friend, Marshall Ratliff did not play "When the Roll is Called Up Yonder" as the condemned man took his final steps through the Green Door.

Chapter 15
Santa's Insanity

Another Crazy Plan

Even though his date for the chair was still unknown, from the moment of Henry Helms' execution, Marshall Ratliff's behavior changed drastically. As if the crazy baton had been passed his way, Ratliff began to mumble, twitch, and have difficulty moving his hands and feet.

On October 23, 1929, after 22 months on Death Row, Ratliff's mother filed paperwork for a sanity hearing on her son's behalf. According to her petition, Marshall Ratliff "had become insane on the subject of religion" and incessantly muttered, "Lord have mercy on my soul." While the petition also mentions that Ratliff was "hit on the head many years ago," Rilla's main claim was that the "the parade of doomed men, stretched over a period of 21 months had driven him insane."

Shortly after, Ratliff was sent back to Eastland to await trial, not for a sanity hearing, however, but for car theft and additional armed robbery charges.

DEATH MARCH OF 15 INSANITY PLEA OF SANTA CLAUS BANDIT

Austin American Statesman, Oct 24, 1929

An Overcrowded Jail

At the time, Eastland's head jailer, Edward Paxton "Pack" Kilborn, had his hands full. The jail was at maximum capacity, and Ratliff's special needs only compounded his work load. As a favor, Mr. Tom Alexander Jones, known affectionately as "Uncle Tom" agreed to assist Kilborn during this busy time.

When the Huntsville guards delivered Ratliff to Eastland County Jail, Kilborn and Jones were warned he might be faking his condition. After putting Ratliff through several unofficial tests, such as poking him with a pin, moving suddenly as if to stab his eye with a fork, and even letting his body fall to the floor from a full standing position, the jailers concluded that Ratliff's paralysis was not an act.

Meanest Man in Texas

In the cell across from Ratliff was a fellow named Clyde Thompson who, at the tender age of 17, became the youngest man in Texas history to receive the death penalty. In later years, Thompson also became known as "the meanest man in Texas," but that's another story.

Like everyone else, Thompson wondered if Ratliff's behavior was an elaborate act or the real deal. After witnessing Ratliff defecate on his bedding, then turn around and eat it, Thompson became just as convinced as his jailers that the man had truly gone crazy.

As always, Rilla Carter visited often, although Ratliff seemed oblivious to his mother's presence. It must have broken her heart.

MOTHER CONDEMNED MAN ASKS REMOVAL FROM DEATH CELL

"SANTA CLAUS" OF CISCO BANK ROBBERY FACES DEATH IN CHAIR

Corsicana Daily Sun, Dec 20, 1928

Pack Kilborn (photo courtesy of Sheriff Wayne Bradford at Eastland County Jail)

Tragic Mistake

On Monday November 18, 1929 a limp and unresponsive Ratliff was spoon-fed yet another dinner. Afterwards, Jones stayed behind to help Ratliff use the chamber pot, while Kilborn continued his duties elsewhere. A few minutes later, Jones tucked Ratliff into bed and walked off to finish up for the night. It's not clear why, whether it was an oversight or extreme casualness due to Ratliff's paralysis, but for some reason, Jones neglected to lock Ratliff's jail cell.

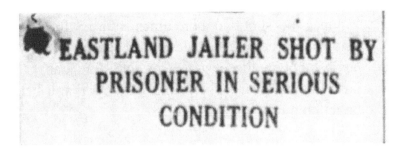

EASTLAND JAILER SHOT BY PRISONER IN SERIOUS CONDITION

Vernon Daily Record, Nov 19, 1929

Ratliff Seizes the Moment

Jones had barely turned the corner when Ratliff seized his chance. As Clyde Thompson watched in surprise, Ratliff leapt from his cot, donned a pair of slippers, and walked out of his cell. Seeing Thompson's startled expression, Ratliff paused briefly to hold a finger up to his lips. Thompson nodded silently in return, hoping that Ratliff would find the keys and let him go, as well.

Ratliff slipped downstairs and tried to escape. Both doors, however, were locked from the inside. He rummaged through Kilborn's desk, but instead of keys, he found a .38 Colt revolver. Ratliff grabbed the gun, ran upstairs, and demanded the keys from Uncle Tom Jones. When the jailer refused, Ratliff shot him at point-blank range. A struggle ensued, and the two men tumbled down the stairs.

Jones Hears the Ruckus

Jones was shot two more times before Kilborn made it to the scene and tackled Ratliff. Kilborn was very nearly shot in the ensuing struggle, but managed to push the gun away. The ceiling of the jail still bears a bullet hole from this incident.

Vernon Daily Record, Nov 19, 1929

Kilborn's family had living quarters in the jailhouse, so when they heard the ruckus, they came running. As the two men grappled, Kilborn's family could only watch helplessly through a small window on the jailhouse door because it was locked from the inside. After a lengthy struggle, Kilborn knocked Ratliff unconscious with the butt of the pistol.

Chapter 16
The Lynching of Santa Claus

Angry Mob in Eastland

The following day, as word of Ratliff's violent actions spread, a crowd slowly gathered near the Eastland County Jail. Some later claimed the KKK used a phone tree to gather support, but this has not been proven.

Although hospital reports for Uncle Tom Jones were optimistic, by nightfall folks began calling out, "We want Santa Claus!" As the crowd swelled and the angry shouts continued, Pack Kilborn stepped outside to calm things down. Unfortunately, the crowd was too worked up. Instead of dispersing, a group of men tackled the jailer, stole his keys, and rushed inside.

Minutes later, the mob shoved Marshall Ratliff out the jail's side door. The crowd cheered as the naked man was dragged down the street. A rope with a noose was tossed over a wire between two light poles behind the Majestic Theatre, which ironically enough, was showing a play entitled "The Noose" at the time.

The angry mob slipped the knot around Ratliff's neck and yanked him into the air to more cheers from the crowd. Moments later, the rope snapped and Ratliff fell to the ground, gasping for breath. A small group of men were sent for a new rope.

While awaiting their return, the lynch mob decided to make it a double feature, using Clyde Thompson as the second act. As Thompson anxiously paced his cell, the mob tried every key on the jailer's set. Even though Thompson knew his keys were kept at the courthouse down the street, he still feared they would get his cell open. The men finally gave up, but swore to return the next day.

Corsicana Semi-Weekly Light, Nov 22, 1929

Second Try with a New Rope

Around 9:30 p.m. a new, and much stronger, rope arrived. As Ratliff was hoisted into the air, his final words were, "Forgive me, boys."

Although still conscious when the lynching

occurred, Uncle Tom Jones died the following morning. Word of the mob's actions reached Jones on his deathbed, but reports are mixed when it comes to his reaction. Some quote him as saying that he was glad to know Ratliff was dead, while others have him calling it a shameful act. Uncle Tom's family claims the jailer would never endorse mob violence, so that seems most likely.

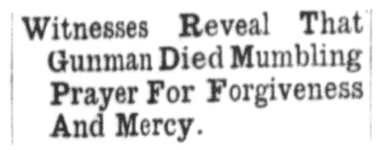

Witnesses Reveal That Gunman Died Mumbling Prayer For Forgiveness And Mercy.

El Paso Times, Nov 21, 1929

Rilla's Final Efforts

Upon learning of Jones' death, Rilla Carter sent his widow a sympathy card expressing sorrow for her loss and remorse for her son's behavior. She also sent a telegram to Governor Moody asking for her son, Lee, to be released for his brother's funeral, but her request was denied.

To appease curiosity seekers, Ratliff's corpse was displayed in the window of Barrow Furniture Company. Before Mrs. Carter could make it to Eastland, thousands of people viewed her son's embalmed body.

Although we balk at this idea now, in those days furniture stores often specialized in casket-making, and by extension, the mortuary business. Even so, after a couple days, Judge Davenport ordered Ratliff's corpse removed from public view.

Final Irony for Santa

Marshall Ratliff's body was taken to Fort Worth, where it was buried in an unmarked grave in Mt. Olivet Cemetery on November 24, 1929. To this day, his final resting place bears no headstone or marker.

In a strange twist of fate, shortly before Ratliff's funeral, a holiday parade featuring a jolly St. Nick passed right by the funeral parlor as if to bestow a final touch of irony upon the infamous Santa Claus bank robber.

Make Believe Santa Claus Passes Before Ratliff Funeral Service

Austin American Statesman, Nov 24, 1929

Undercover Mourners

Several undercover policemen attended Ratliff's

funeral, although not out of sympathy. Since Robert Hill looked upon Rilla Carter as a mother figure, and he was currently on the lam, cops hoped he would make an appearance at his friend's funeral. Hill was not seen at the service, but was captured soon after and returned to prison.

COPS SEARCH BURIAL CROWD

Brownsville Herald, Nov 24, 1929

Greene Blurs Facts Yet Again

Newspapers also noted that Ratliff's sweetheart, Florence Herron, attended his funeral. Although A.C. Greene's book mentions that Ratliff's sweetheart attended his funeral, he fails to tell readers that she is one of Josephine Herron's daughters. As always, anytime the narrative touches upon Josephine Herron and her family, Greene tiptoes around the subject.

Grand Jury Comes Up Empty

In response to Marshall Ratliff's lynching, District Attorney Joe H. Jones prepared a list of 75 people to call before a grand jury. As Uncle Tom's nephew, Jones certainly had a personal interest in the matter. Even so, this list of names was never made public and the matter quietly disappeared. No one was ever brought to justice for Marshall Ratliff's death, which is now considered the last mob lynching in Texas history.

Embarrassment Lingers Over Tragic Past

The lynching of the Santa Claus bank robber did little to improve the reputation of West Texas in the eyes of those who lived elsewhere, even in other parts of the state. Mob violence is hardly a source of civic pride, and Eastland was no exception.

Nearly a century later, embarrassment over this incident lingers. Some historians I approached, especially those living in Eastland, made it clear they were not interested in sharing details about this tragic tale, nor did they understand why I was writing this book.

Chapter 17
Justice for All?

Dead Bank Robber Reward

It would now appear that all criminals involved in the Santa Claus bank robbery were either deceased or safely behind bars, and that is exactly what most accounts leave readers thinking. In my early research, that was my conclusion, too. Now, however, I'm not so sure. I will circle back to that, but first, let's talk about that Dead Bank Robber Reward.

With so many shots fired from so many guns, and only one bandit mortally wounded at the scene of the crime, you may wonder who got the $5000 Dead Bank Robber Reward for shooting Lewis Davis during the Cisco robbery.

As early as December 28, 1927, there was talk of dividing the robber reward for Lewis Davis between the surviving family members of Chief Bedford and Deputy Carmichael, since both men lost their lives during the robbery. Even Mrs. B.P. Blasingame felt entitled to a piece of the pie, since she is the one who originally alerted police to the crime in progress.

The Texas State Bankers Association, however,

hesitated to award the money until someone could definitively prove they had fired the killing shots. In the end, the only person rewarded for their actions during the Cisco robbery was Woody Harris, who received an engraved gold pocket watch from the bank's insurance company.

BANKERS WILL PAY REWARD

FORT WORTH, Dec. 27. — (AP) — As soon as definite proof can be established as to who fired the shots which killed the two men who took part in the robbery of the First National bank of Cisco Friday, the Texas Bankers' association will pay the two rewards of $5000 each, W. M. Massie, president of the association, said today.

Austin American Statesman, Dec 27, 1927

Robber Reward Causes Controversy

The Dead Bank Robber Reward of Texas generated a lot of controversy, and not just in Cisco. Eager vigilantes sometimes took a "shoot first, ask questions later" approach with innocent strangers with tragic consequences.

In one incident, a man out scouting for oil was chased all over West Texas because locals didn't recognize his car and assumed he must be a bank robber.

One of the worst cases, however, occurred on December 23, 1927, the same day as the Santa Claus bank robbery. (See? I told you there were a lot of robberies every day in Texas during the 1920s!)

In this despicable incident, a deputy sheriff and his friend from the West Texas town of Wink picked up four Mexicans who were looking for work. After driving the men to the nearby town of Stanton, the deputy and his friend told the men to wait in front of a bank while they ran a quick errand.

Meanwhile, a church across town caught fire, conveniently diverting emergency personnel and many citizens. While others fought the fire, the deputy and his friend rushed back to the bank and shot the Mexicans, killing two of them. Although the shooters claimed a bank robbery was in progress, the truth soon came to light.

In response to incidents like this, citizens, law enforcement agents, and politicians pressed for a change in the Dead Bank Robber Reward's wording so that rather than offering $5,000 "for the delivery of dead bank robbers and no other kind," it would say "for capture and conviction of bank robbers." Besides providing fodder for many arguments, the wording remained the same.

While it's impossible to know how many bank robbers were deterred by the Dead Bank Robber Reward in Texas, it stayed on the books until 1964.

BANDIT BOUNTY CRITICIZED

Dan Suggests Change in Reward.

Texas Gov. Dan Moody was among those to suggest changes to the Dead Bank Robber Reward to avoid abuse. (Austin American Statesman, Dec 31, 1927)

Chapter 18
A Mystery Remains

Pity for Robert Hill

Remember Freda Stroebel? She was the clerk Ratliff used as a human shield as he exited the bank during the Cisco robbery shootout. In an interview many years later, Stroebel remarked, "If you go through something like [the Santa Claus bank robbery], you're inclined to think that the bandits got what they deserved. They didn't show anyone any mercy. But I always kind of felt sorry for Robert Hill."

So what exactly happened to Mr. Hill a.k.a. "the boy who never had a chance"?

Hill Tried for Murder

Although originally elated to receive a 99-year sentence instead of the death penalty, Hill was not out of the woods yet. After a jailbreak from a prison farm, in 1931 Hill was shipped back to Eastland to stand trial for the for the murder of Chief Bedford.

Once again, Hill managed to avoid the death sentence. You would think this close call would have a sobering effect on him, but Hill managed to break out of jail two more times before he finally settled down.

After one escape, Hill left a cheeky note behind reading, "If you want to find me, you will have to come to Paris, France." (Since we have a town named Paris here in Texas, this distinction was necessary.)

Last Survivor Of Cisco Bandits To Go to Trial

Denton Record Chronicle, Feb 21, 1931

Robert Hill's Slippery Reputation

Robert Hill's jailbreaks were so notorious that a North Texas criminal once dropped his name to scare a victim. In 1941, a woman named Leona Langsford picked up a hitchhiker near Mineral Wells. Claiming to be Robert Hill, the man pulled a pair of pistols and demanded that she continue driving to Weatherford,

"I'm ready to shoot it out," he told her, "because if they get me it'll mean death anyway." Rather than comply, Langsford pulled into a filling station, tossed her keys out the window and screamed bloody murder. Her abductor ran off, and a search for Robert Hill began.

He was quickly found. It was pretty easy this time,

JAILBREAKERS YET AT LARGE

Six Escape Prison Here Early Wednesday by Sawing Bars

Tyler Morning Telegraph, Jun 16, 1932

since the real Robert Hill was safely behind bars in the Texas State Penitentiary. His impersonator, on the other hand, was never found.

Despite all these jailbreaks, Robert Hill was eventually released from prison in 1948 and received a full pardon on August 17, 1964.

Robert Hill's Secret Rendezvous

While in prison, Robert Hill sent letters of apology to at least two of the Santa Claus bank robbery victims, Laverne Comer (one of the little girls at the bank) and Woody Harris (the teen who foiled their first carjacking.) It is not known whether Hill stayed in touch with Rilla Carter, but I wouldn't be surprised

*Robert Hill as he appeared in later life. (photo
courtesy of the Conrad Hilton Center)*

since he mentioned in court that she was the first
person in his life to show him any kindness.

New Name for a New Life

After his official release, Hill was granted
permission to change his name. He moved to either
Odessa or Midland, joined a church, got married,
became a step-father, and stayed out of trouble with
the law for the rest of his life.

According to A.C. Greene, he married a gal named
Gladys who was the postmistress in a small West
Texas town. However, given Greene's penchant for
pseudonyms, I rather doubt that is her real name and
occupation.

Even after prison, Robert Hill remained in close
contact with Woody Harris. Perhaps, after spending so

Harris Disagrees With Book's Version of the Robbery

Abilene Reporter-News, Dec 18, 1977

much of his life in institutions, Hill's crime victims were the closest thing he had to family.

Over the years, Hill and Harris became such good friends that on December 23, 1977 they held a secret rendezvous to commemorate the 50th anniversary of the Santa Claus bank robbery. They wouldn't tell anyone where they went, although it definitely was *not* First National Bank in Cisco, Texas. According to Woody Harris, "He doesn't get much of a kick out of banks."

In 1962, the president of Cisco's First National Bank, James P. McCracken, who collected memorabilia from the notorious robbery, spoke with Robert Hill and revealed that, "We believe he will write his side of the story some day, when it can no longer hurt his family."

Author Befriends Santa Claus Bandit

Robert Hill never penned his memoirs, but A.C. Greene refers to him as a consultant for his 1972 book, *The Santa Claus Bank Robbery.* Over the years, the two men became good friends. Greene even dedicates *The Santa Claus Bank Robbery* to Robert, or Bob, as the author refers to him.

Despite their close friendship, A.C. Greene makes it clear that he most certainly does not condone Hill's criminal behavior. He did, however, respect the manner in which Hill turned his life around.

As for Hill, when Greene asked him to sign his personal copy of the book, the ex-con wrote, "I hope this book will cause young men to see crime cannot pay."

I think it's wonderful that Greene had Hill to consult. In fact, I envy his access to such a close source of information.

Greene even claims that in later life when people would ask Robert Hill questions about the infamous bank robbery, the ex-con would pull his copy of Greene's book off the shelf and flip through it as a reference!

Woody Harris Weighs In

In addition to Robert Hill, Woody Harris also befriended Marshall Ratliff's son, DeArman. Surprisingly, Woody Harris was not a fan of *The Santa Claus Bank Robbery*. When a reporter asked him about the A.C. Greene's book in 1977, Woody scoffed.

"It's all a damned lie," he said. "I wouldn't have it in my home."

The article goes on to claim that, according to Woody, neither Robert Hill nor Marshall Ratliff's sons like the book, either!

Lingering Question

Unfortunately, since Robert Hill, A.C. Greene, Woody Harris, and Ratliff's sons have all passed away, it's impossible for me to ask them for clarification.

Personally, I enjoyed reading A.C. Greene's book. And from what I can tell from my own research, Greene's account of Woody's heroic actions during the getaway is an accurate portrayal of events.

All opinions aside, one question remains: Why did A.C. Greene purposely obscure so many connections between the Herron family and the bandits?

Reviewing the Evidence

It may not seem like a big deal for A.C. Greene to change a few names here and there. However, when you make a list of his discrepancies, they really add up.

Greene uses pseudonyms for the following:
- Josephine Herron, the bandits' landlady
- Frances Herron, her husband
- Marion Herron, her daughter
- Minnie Fox, Lewis Davis's sister and Henry Helms' sister-in-law.
- Sam Fox, Minnie's husband
- Other member of the Fox family.

Key facts Greene fails to mention:
- Henry Helms and Lewis Davis are brothers-in-law
- Josephine Herron was charged with being an

accessory after the fact to the murder of Chief Bedford.
- Josephine Herron's daughter (Florence) attended Ratliff's funeral
- Marshall Ratliff was dating Florence Herron,
- Josephine Herron's hair appeared dyed when they arrested her.
- Josephine Herron claimed that Helms ran a "dope ring."
- The Herron residence was under police surveillance.
- Wichita Falls police found loot from an earlier bank robbery in Josephine Herron's backyard.

What's the Motive?

One could argue that A.C. Greene simply wanted to protect the Herron family's privacy. If so, why didn't he change everyone's names? I really wish I knew.

Even if Josephine Herron was not the "blonde-headed woman" who shot down Chief Bedford, it seems likely that she knew much more about the bandits than she let on. To me, it seems highly probable that she was an accessory to their crimes.

A.C. Greene had a long and illustrious career as a newspaper man. As a professional journalist, I am sure he knew what he was doing when he gave pseudonyms to Josephine Herron and those close to her. But exactly what were his motives? To me, that is perhaps the most enduring mystery of all surrounding this strange-but-true tale of greed and crime in West Texas.

Chapter 19
The Aftermath

What About Everyone Else?

In the previous chapter, I mentioned that Woody Harris, the teen who foiled the bandits' carjacking attempt, lived out his days in the little West Texas town of Rising Star, where he owned an appliance store. But what about everyone else?

While I do not yet know the fate of everyone involved in the Santa Claus bank robbery, here is a smattering of what I've learned, so far.

Remember Francis Blasingame, the little girl who followed Santa into the bank? The Blasingame family eventually moved to Dallas, where she eventually married and spent the rest of her life.

Marion Olson, the law student who took a bullet to the thigh during the bank shootout, healed up and graduated from Harvard Law School. He eventually settled in San Antonio where he became a successful attorney.

Lela Latch, the girl who chatted with the bandit Santa on his way to the bank, eventually married, becoming Lela Latch Lloyd. She taught school in Cisco, and a museum bearing her name is now in the building which formerly housed Cisco's City Hall and police department in 1927.

Sheriff Silas "Si" Bradford later became a Texas Ranger. As of this writing, Si's descendant, Wayne Bradford, is the current sheriff of Eastland County. He has even turned the historic jail house into a small museum. In fact, if you contact Sheriff Bradford in advance, he will give you a private tour of the cells which once housed the Santa Claus bandits. (See   for details.)

Ratliff's Sons

Remember Marshall Ratliff's two little boys? I didn't find much about Dane Ratliff, but his brother DeArman "Pat" Fields Ratliff was quite a character.

Ratliff's sons were sent to live with relatives in Cross Cut, Texas, where they grew up on a dairy farm. From milking 25 cows morning and night, Pat Ratliff developed incredibly strong hands. By his late teens, Pat performed shows of strength that included ripping a quarter in half and prying horseshoes apart – using only his bare hands!

As an adult, Pat moved to Oklahoma and became so well-known for his talents that Robert Duval spent time with him to get a feel for portraying a cowboy in the movie "Lonesome Dove."

Pat became good friends with the actor, and Duval often flew him to visit his ranch in Virginia. Duval also got Ratliff a small speaking part in a movie he directed called "The Apostle."

Pat Ratliff didn't want much to do with Hollywood,

but he often journeyed to Oklahoma City to speak to state legislators.

"I think it is important that someone tell them how important our way of life is," according to Pat. "If they had their way, there are a lot of people who would do away with hunting, fishing, rodeos, and cockfighting."

Pat also raised roosters, and once sold some to Vincente Fox when he was president of Mexico. When Pat Ratliff passed away in 2008, Wilford Brimley was an honorary pall bearer. I wasn't able to find any quotes where he spoke of his father's criminal past, but it doesn't seem to have held him back during his life.

Billy Smith a.k.a. Banjo Billy (photo courtesy of Billy Smith)

Santa Claus Bank Robbery Musical

Cisco's First National Bank moved to a new location in 1982. In the years since, the old bank building housed several different businesses. As of this writing, the site of the infamous heist serves as prop storage for a musical entitled "The Great Santa Claus Bank Robbery."

That's right, folks. While rumors of a movie version of the Santa Claus bank robbery have been circulating since the early 1970s, a bluegrass musical based upon the event debuted in 2005. Playwright Billy Smith penned the show while working at Cisco College as its director of performing arts. Unfortunately, Billy Smith retired and the musical has been shelved – at least for now.

When I spoke to Billy about "The Great Santa Claus Bank Robbery" he described it as a light-hearted romp that pokes fun at the greed on both sides of the chase. Smith composed 14 original songs for the dinner show, which includes audience participation, and sounds like a lot of fun.

And yes, Smith's play includes the mysterious blonde-headed woman. Called "Lady Luck" in his version, the audience can see and hear her, but the bandits cannot. I sure hope someone produces the show again soon.

Brochure for Billy Smith's musical (photo courtesy of Billy Smith)

You Can Listen to the Songs

The following link will let you hear the songs from Billy Smith's show called the "Great Santa Claus Bank Robbery":

http://bit.ly/SantaRobberSongs

Cisco's Other Claims to Fame

As for the town of Cisco, the population has fallen sharply since the late 1920's. Today, only 4,000 people live there, but it is a thriving little town and well worth visiting.

I can't help but wonder what might have happened if Marshall Ratliff had made better use of his cleverness. It's not like you couldn't start in Cisco and then go far. Sylvan Goldman, who invented the shopping cart, is from Cisco, as are actress Jean Porter, and Dash Croft of the 1970s rock band "Seals & Croft." Speaking of musicians, Lawrence Welk had his very first paying gig in Cisco.

Down the street from the First National Bank is a brick building that was once known as The Mobley Hotel. This was the first of many owned by famous hotelier, Conrad Hilton. Cisco's Avenue D, which still serves as its main drag, is now named "Conrad Hilton Boulevard" in his honor. The Mobley Hotel building now houses the Cisco Chamber of Commerce and the Conrad Hilton Museum. (You've got to wonder if Conrad's infamous party girl descendant, Paris Hilton, was actually named after Paris, Texas and not the one in France.)

Strong Women

Readers sometimes ask who my favorite character is from the *Santa Claus Bank Robbery*. They are often surprised to hear that the people who fascinate me the most are Rilla Carter and Mrs. B.P. Blasingame.

I have great respect for Mrs. Blasingame's decision to race through the bank with her little girl despite warnings from the bandits that they would shoot. If she hadn't warned police, who knows how things would have played out?

I also feel tremendous empathy for Rilla Carter, Marshall Ratliff's devoted mother. Despite his criminal inclinations, Rilla never gave up on her son. I admire how she took it upon herself to learn the intricacies of the legal system and when I read about her letter of condolence to the jailer's widow after her son's attempted jailbreak, I was quite moved.

So although this story focuses on the tragic shenanigans of four male criminals, the outcome was strongly shaped by the bravery of those two women.

Still Searching

That wraps up my version of the strange- but-true events surrounding the Santa Claus bank robbery at Cisco's First National Bank. I hope you enjoyed reading it as much as I enjoyed the research and writing.

Honestly, though? I'm still searching newspaper archives, talking to locals, and keeping an eye out for any trace of that mysterious blonde-headed woman. If I find anything, I will let you know!

Places of Interest

Related Places of Interest

Maybe it's the travel writer in me, but I couldn't end this book without sharing some places in Cisco and Eastland related to the Santa Claus bank robbery that are well worth checking out in person. When you visit, be sure and tell them Tui sent you:

Cisco's First National Bank Building

You can't go inside the old bank building, which is currently owned by playwright, Billy Smith, but the alley remains. A trip here really helps visualize how the shootout went down, and to see where Mrs. B.P. Blasingame and little Frances ran to alert police.

Plus, you can check out the Texas State Historical plaque and the snazzy neon sign for "The Great Santa Claus Bank Robbery" musical while you are there.

address: 418 Conrad Hilton Blvd Cisco, TX 76437
website: https://www.prosperitybankusa.com/loc-cisco.aspx

The bank robbery site with a good look at the "getaway alley" in 2015. (photo by the author)

Prosperity Bank - Mural

A few blocks down from the robbery site, you'll find Prosperity Bank. This is where you can see a 45-foot-long mural by the late western artist Randy Steffen depicting the history of Cisco. Right smack dab in the middle, you can see the Santa Claus bank robbery in progress. Every time I've visited, the bank tellers have been friendly and informative.

address: 116 W 7th St, Cisco, TX 76437
website: http://www.rcgates.com/museum/

Prosperity bank mural by Randy Steffen (photo taken by author)

Lela Latch Lloyd Museum

The Lela Latch Lloyd Museum is housed in Cisco's old city hall building, built in 1915. After visiting the old First National Bank building, if you walk up the alley and turn right, you are taking the same route as Mrs. B.P. Blasingame and her daughter when they alerted police to the Santa Claus bank robbery.

As you probably guessed, this museum takes its name from the college girl who shook hands with Santa shortly before he robbed the bank. Her married name was Lela Latch Lloyd and she later became a local schoolteacher, historian, and author.

Curated by Dr. Duane K. Hale, the The Lela Latch Lloyd Museum is chock full of memorabilia pertaining to the Santa Claus bank robbery, including an actual poster describing the Dead Bank Robber Reward, a drainpipe with a bullet hole from the shootout, and pistols used by the bandits.

Dr. Hale is extremely knowledgeable about West Texas history and his booklet called the Santa Claus Bank Robbery and Its Effect on Eye Witnesses was very helpful to me.

In addition to the Santa Claus bank robbery, the Lela Latch Lloyd Museum includes a wide variety of items pertaining to West Texas history, including Native American artifacts, relics from Spanish and Mexican occupation, items from early settlers, and much more. The museum is free to the public, but there is a donation box. Be generous!

address: 116 W 7th St, Cisco, TX 76437
website: http://www.rcgates.com/museum/

Conrad Hilton Center

The Conrad Hilton Center is another must- see for those interested in the Santa Claus bank robbery. In addition to numerous photos, news clippings, and exhibits, curator John Waggoner has video clips from several shows mentioning the Santa Claus bank robbery on TV, including The Travel Channel's "Mysteries at the Museum."

address: 309 Conrad Hilton Blvd, Cisco, TX 76437
website: http://www.ciscotx.com

The rope used to lynch "Santa" is on display at the Eastland County Jail Museum. (photo taken by the author)

Eastland County Jail Museum

Sheriff Wayne Bradford curates a wonderful little museum in this historic county jail. Items on display include a gun belt worn by Marshall Ratliff and the rope that lynched him. You can also see the bullet hole in the ceiling from Ratliff's struggle with jailers, the cells where inmates were kept, and the names of Robert Hill and Henry Helms scratched into the metal walls of their cells. Free tours of this museum are available by appointment only. The graffiti they scratched into their cell walls is still there! Bradford does an excellent job of reenacting the violent jailbreak that led to Ratliff's lynching, and has kept some other artifacts from the crime, too. It's well

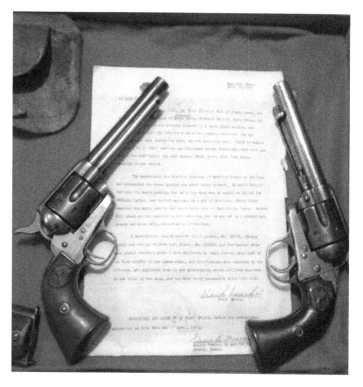

Marshall Ratliff's pistols on display. (courtesy of the Lela Latch Lloyd Museum)

worth arranging a tour.

address: 210 W. White St, Eastland, TX 76448
website: http://www.eastlandfoundation.com/

Majestic Theatre

While manager Rhyne Hobbs gives interesting tours of this historic facility, you can get a big dose of history simply taking in a movie or performance here. The Majestic Theatre has a gorgeous marquee, a 1953 popcorn maker, affordable concessions, and an excellent collection of vintage movie posters.

address: 108 N Lamar St, Eastland, TX 76448
website: http://www.majesticeastland.com/

Memorial for the Santa Claus Lynching

Behind the Majestic Theatre and across the street from the Eastland County Jail you will find a small marker resembling a headstone at the corner of White and Lamar. Engraved in the marker is a brief account of the lynching of the Santa Claus bank robber.

The utility poles used to hang Marshall Ratliff have since been removed, but you can still get an idea of how this moment in history played out by standing here and looking over at the jail. Ratliff was dragged out of the white metal side door that you see in the old section of the jail.

address: 108 N Lamar St, Eastland, TX 76448
website: none

Allen Family Style Meals

The town of Sweetwater is a fair drive from Cisco and Eastland and it has nothing to do with the Santa Claus bank robbery per se. Even so, I'd feel remiss if I didn't include the address and website for the little restaurant that kicked off my fascination with this

*Memorial for Ratliff's mob lynching. You can see the Old
Eastland County Jail in the background. (photo by author)*

strange-but-true Texas tale!

address: 1301 E Broadway, Sweetwater, TX 79556
website: https://www.facebook.com/AllensFamilyStyleMeals/

Let's Stay in Touch

Thanks for reading!

Thank you for reading my book. I hope it kept you entertained and inspired your curiosity. If you enjoyed the *Santa Claus Bank Robbery: A True-Crime Saga in Texas*, please leave a review for it on Amazon.com and/or Goodreads. Reviews help other readers make up their minds. It all adds up, and your help is appreciated!

While you're there, check out my other books, which currently include: Understanding Cemetery Symbols (a guide to historic graveyards), 100 Things to Do in Dallas - Fort Worth Before You Die (a playful bucket list of travel ideas), Paranormal Texas (a travel guide to haunted places in North Texas) and more!

Full list of books here

That's only a partial list of my published books, and I have several more on the way! To see a full list of my books, search for "Tui Snider" on Amazon, or drop by my website, TuiSnider.com. I write books and articles

Tui Snider has lots more books on the way! © *Tui Snider*

about offbeat travel, haunted places, historic cemetery symbols, the 1897 airship mystery, weird history, and more!

Presentations & Speaking Events

I enjoy giving presentations and am available to speak at book fairs, conferences, libraries, bookstores – you name it! If you know of an upcoming event needing presenters, drop me a line. Even if you don't, please tell your local library and bookstore about me. To see a list of upcoming events, interviews, and appearances, visit TuiSnider.com.

Contact the Author

And lastly, I truly enjoy hearing from readers. Do

you have information about the mysterious blonde-headed woman or any other ideas to share? Would you like to say hi? To get in touch, drop by TuiSnider.com or give me a howdy on social media. I'm especially active on Twitter, Facebook (please give my author page a like!), and Instagram. To reach me directly, simply email TuiSnider@gmail.com.

Thanks again and I look forward to hearing from you!

Further Reading

Books

Baker, T. Lindsay, (2011), *Gangster Tour of Texas*, Texas A&M University Press, College Station, TX

Coley, Julie Williams, (2009), *How Did They Die? Murders in Northern Texas 1892-1927*, CreateSpace, USA

Greene, A.C., (1972), *The Santa Claus Bank Robbery*, University of North Texas Press, Denton, TX

Hale, Duane Kendall, (2000), *The Santa Claus Bank Robbery*, Eastland & Callahan County Publishers, Eastland, TX

Umphrey, Don, (1984), *The Meanest Man in Texas*, Quarry Press, Dallas, TX

Wooley, Lee D., (1958), *The Santa Claus Bank Robbery*, Longhorn Press, Cisco, TX

Yadon, Laurence J., and Anderson, Dan, (2009), *Ten Deadly Texans*, Pelican Publishing Company, Gretna, LA

Newspapers

Abilene Morning News
Abilene Reporter News
Amarillo Daily News
Amarillo Globe-Times
Austin American Statesman
Austin American Sun
Battle Creek Enquirer
Berkeley Daily Gazette
Brownsville Herald
Chicago Tribune
Cisco Daily News
Corsicana Daily Sun
Corsicana Semi-Weekly Light
Daily Sentinel
Dallas Morning News
Denton Record Chronicle
Eastland Telegram
El Paso Herald
Evening Independent
Fort Worth Star Telegram
Kansas City Star
Lincoln Star
Longview News-Journal
Los Angeles Times
Louisville Courier-Journal
Marshall News Messenger
McAllen Daily Press
News-Herald
Rochester Democrat and Chronicle
San Angelo Standard Times
Sarasota Herald Tribune
Springfield Leader
Taylor Daily Press
Tyler Morning Telegraph
Vernon Daily Record
Victoria Advocate
Weatherford Democrat
Wichita Daily times

Websites

Ancestry.com: http://www.ancestry.com/

Conrad Hilton Center: http://www.ciscotx.com

Eastland Community Foundation: http://www.eastlandfoundation.com/

Find a Grave: http://www.findagrave.com/

Graham Police Department: http://www.grahampd.com/

Officer Down Memorial Page: http://www.odmp.org/

Old Fulton New York Postcards: http://www.fultonhistory.com/

Lela Latch Lloyd Museum: http://www.rcgates.com/museum

Majestic Theatre of Eastland: http://www.majesticeastland.com/

Portal to Texas History: http://texashistory.unt.edu/

REH: Two Gun Raconteur: http://www.rehtwogunraconteur.com/

Roadside America: http://www.roadsideamerica.com/

Texas Escapes Online Magazine: http://www.texasescapes.com/

Texas State Historical Association: http://www.tshaonline.org/

Texas State Library and Archives: https://www.tsl.texas.gov

Made in the USA
Monee, IL
15 January 2021

57667009R00085